EXTRA-SPECIAL **CROCKERY POT** RECIPES

REVISED EDITION

Lou Seibert Pappas

BRISTOL PUBLISHING ENTERPRISES
San Leandro, California

A Nitty Gritty® Cookbook

Cover design: Frank Paredes
Cover photography: John Benson
Food stylist: Suzanne Carreiro
Illustrator: James Balkovek

Printed in the United States of America.

ISBN 1-55867-107-2

CONTENTS

INTRODUCTION

When the first edition of this book was published in 1975, electric crockery pots were a relative newcomer in the kitchen. Now, nearly 20 years later, this useful appliance continues to be a popular one. Once you have used a slow electric cooker, it is easy to understand why. It's like having a "genie" at home cooking while you're away. When you arrive home, delicious food is waiting and there's no preparation mess to clean up. That was all done earlier in the day! It creates a note of serenity in the kitchen. You are free to relax for a few minutes, and there's even time for an apéritif. Dinner waits without fear of scorching or drying out.

An often overlooked feature of the versatile crockery pot is that it is also a marvelous food warmer/server. It is excellent for buffets and potluck dinner parties. The low temperature setting allows you to keep previously cooked food warm so guests can help themselves. It is ideal for heat-and-serve dishes.

Because the main crockery pot concept calls for long cooking, it forces the master of the kitchen to organize in advance. It means you get set for dinner early in the day rather than relying on something fast in the evening. Many working parents make some of the necessary preparations, such as cutting up meat and organizing the other ingredients, the evening before. Putting the recipe together the next morning takes only a few minutes. The crockery pot is turned on and dinner is on its way.

Slow cooking, made possible by the low temperature, is the key to the fine flavor, juiciness and lack of shrinkage you achieve, especially with meats and poultry. Food cooked with this slow method retains more vitamins and minerals, too. Low is about 200°F, or just below boiling, and high is approximately 300°F. In addition to the low temperature, a wrap-around heating system makes this kind of cooking possible. It eliminates the concentration of heat on the bottom of the pot that causes scorching or requires you to be there to stir occasionally. Believe it or not, hollandaise sauce, which curdles so easily, will hold beautifully at a perfect serving temperature for as long as 6 hours!

Even on high, the temperature of crockery pot cookers is not hot enough for browning. When necessary, it is best to do this in a skillet. While it does involve another cooking step, it enhances the flavor immeasurably and is well worth the trouble. Always be sure to rinse the skillet out with a little water, wine or broth after using and add it to the crockery pot so that none of the delicious flavor and color from the pan drippings is lost.

When cooking meat and chicken, there will be a quantity of broth at the finish, since there is almost no evaporation during cooking. If there is time, it is possible to reduce the stock by turning the crockery pot temperature to high, but it is considerably faster to ladle the stock into a saucepan and boil it down. The essence you achieve through reducing the stock is far superior to the double quantity of broth you started with.

Crockery pots do have their limitations when it comes to vegetables, especially green ones, which lose their beautiful bright color and flavor after hours in the crockery pot. Faster, last-minute cooking is better for them.

I have updated existing recipes to reduce fat and have included many new recipes in this edition, as well as a new chapter on pasta and casseroles, reflecting the changes in eating habits that have occurred since earlier editions were written. I hope this newly revised international collection of recipes will please you.

Lou Seibert Pappas
Palo Alto, California

SOUPS

Soup has played an important part in the diets of people all over the world. No wonder! It is nourishing, inexpensive, easy to prepare, endless in its variety and enjoyed by people of all ages. Soup is a natural for crockery pot cooking. The low temperature is ideal for capturing the mellow flavor that is only achieved through slow cooking.

Many of the recipes included here are full meal soups from various parts of the world, all of which are improved by slow cooking. Others are first course soups merely heated and kept warm, such as the savory *Maritata*, which should not be allowed to simmer. A crockery pot serves both purposes well.

Regardless of the kind of soup, a crockery-lined cooker is perfect for both cooking and serving.

MARITATA

Maritata is a soup for celebrations. In Italy it is the wedding soup. Enjoy it anytime as a rich first course to begin a chicken, veal or fish dinner.

4 cups homemade or canned low fat chicken broth
1 cup dry white wine
½ cup coil vermicelli
4 egg yolks
1 cup (½ pt.) heavy cream
1 cup (4 oz.) grated Monterey Jack cheese
½ cup freshly shredded Parmesan cheese,
  or Romano cheese

Heat broth and wine in the crockery pot on high (300°). When simmering, drop in vermicelli. Cook until firm to the bite (*al dente*), but not too soft or chewy, about 10 minutes. Beat egg yolks until thick and light in color. Beat in cream and cheeses. Ladle a spoonful of hot broth into egg mixture and blend. Slowly blend into broth in crockery pot. Reduce heat to low (200°); stir occasionally until heated through.

VINEYARD SOUP

Here is a delightful first course soup to sip in the garden or living room as a prelude to dinner. Serve in small mugs, Japanese tea cups or small French soufflé dishes.

4 cups homemade or canned low fat beef broth
1 cup dry red wine, or dry sherry
salt and pepper to taste
thin lemon or lime slices for garnish

Heat broth and wine in the crockery pot on high (300°), just until steaming. Season with salt and pepper. Ladle into small mugs. Float a lemon or lime slice in each serving.

MEXICAN CHICKEN CHILE SOUP

Mexican seasonings lend vibrant flavor to this chicken and pasta soup.

6 cups homemade or canned low fat
  chicken broth
1/2 cup vermicelli
3 tbs. vegetable oil
2 chicken breast halves
2 chopped green chile peppers,
  or 1/4 cup salsa

1 tomato, peeled and chopped
2 green onions, finely chopped
1 avocado
chopped fresh cilantro
toasted pumpkin seeds, or sunflower
  seeds

Heat chicken broth in the crockery pot on high (300°), add chicken and cook for 1 1/2 to 2 hours, or until breasts are tender. Remove chicken from broth, allow to cool and cut meat into strips. Break vermicelli into 1/2-inch pieces. In a large skillet, sauté vermicelli in oil until lightly browned. Drain on paper towels and add to simmering stock. Cook until firm to the bite (*al dente*), but not too soft or chewy, about 10 minutes. Stir in chicken, chile peppers, tomato and onions. Heat just until hot through. Peel and dice avocado and place in a small bowl. Mound cilantro and seeds in small bowls. Serve avocado, cilantro and seeds as condiments with soup.

TUSCANY PEASANT SOUP

Serve this hearty soup accompanied by garlic-buttered, toasted French bread. Italian sausages made from turkey meat can be found in most supermarkets.

4 mild Italian sausages, preferably turkey
1 inner stalk celery, diced
3 medium zucchini, or crookneck or summer squash, thinly sliced
1 small onion, chopped
3 cups homemade or canned low fat beef broth

1 can (8 oz.) tomato sauce, or 2 fresh tomatoes, chopped
2 tsp. chopped fresh basil, or ½ tsp. dried
salt and pepper to taste
grated Parmesan cheese, or Romano cheese for garnish

Slice sausages ½-inch thick. In a large skillet, brown sausages (if turkey, first spray skillet with nonstick vegetable spray). Pour off any fat. Add celery, zucchini and onion. Sauté for 2 minutes, stirring. Put broth, tomato sauce and basil into the crockery pot and mix. Heat on high (300°) for 30 minutes. Add sausage-vegetable mixture to crockery pot. Reduce heat to low (200°) and cook for 2 to 3 hours. Add salt and pepper. Ladle into bowls and garnish with grated cheese.

KIT CARSON SOUP

Servings: 6
Cooking time: 9 hours

This soup is claimed to have originated with the famous frontiersman himself.

1 broiler-fryer chicken, about 3 lb., or
  2 turkey drumsticks
1 qt. water
1 onion, quartered
1 stalk celery, chopped
1 clove garlic, minced
1 bay leaf
2 tsp. salt

⅛ tsp. hot red pepper flakes
6 whole black peppercorns
¾ tsp. dried oregano
2 yellow crookneck squash, sliced
1 cup canned garbanzo beans
fresh cilantro, salted sunflower seeds,
  or pine nuts, and 1 avocado, peeled
  and sliced, for garnish

Wash chicken well and place in the crockery pot. Add water, onion, celery, garlic, bay leaf, salt, pepper flakes and peppercorns. Cover and cook on low (200°) for 8 hours, or until tender. Lift chicken from broth and cool. Remove meat from bones and cut into 1-inch cubes. Strain stock and return to crockery pot. Turn heat to high (300°). Add oregano, squash and garbanzo beans. Cover and cook for 1 hour. Add chicken and heat through. Ladle into bowls and sprinkle with cilantro and seeds. Arrange several avocado slices on top of soup in each bowl.

MULLIGATAWNY SOUP

This Indian soup is intended to be a full meal. For company dining, use choice chicken pieces and remove meat from the bones.

1 cup boiling water
1 cup shredded coconut
1 onion, finely chopped
1 carrot, peeled and grated
3 tbs. butter
1 tbs. curry powder
1 broiler-fryer chicken, cut into pieces

4 cups homemade or canned low fat
  chicken broth
2 bay leaves
salt and pepper to taste
hot cooked rice
1 lime, cut into wedges, for garnish
chopped fresh cilantro for garnish

Pour boiling water over coconut and set aside. In a large skillet, sauté onion and carrot in butter until limp and golden. Add curry powder and cook for 3 to 4 minutes. Add chicken and sauté until browned. Transfer to the crockery pot. Drain coconut through a wire strainer. Save liquid and discard coconut. Add coconut liquid, broth and bay leaves to chicken. Season with salt and pepper. Cover crockery pot and cook on high (300°) for 2 to 3 hours, or until chicken is tender. Mound rice in each bowl and ladle in soup. Garnish with lime wedges and cilantro.

BEEF VEGETABLE SOUP

Servings: 8-10
Cooking time: 8-10 hours

A hearty beef vegetable soup makes a fine winter supper. Serve with grated Parmesan cheese and sourdough French bread. Serve pears and cheese for dessert.

2 tbs. olive oil
3 slices beef shank, about 1½ lb.
1 onion, chopped
2 carrots, peeled and chopped
1 stalk celery, chopped
2 qt. homemade or canned low fat beef broth
1 can (16 oz.) stewed tomatoes
salt and pepper to taste
2 tsp. chopped fresh basil, or ½ tsp. dried

(handwritten notes: ½ recipe, cabbage, peas, herbs → noodles, worcestershire)

Heat oil in a large skillet. Brown meat on both sides; remove to the crockery pot. Add onion, carrots and celery to skillet and sauté until limp. Transfer to crockery pot. Add beef broth, tomatoes, salt, pepper and basil. Cover and cook on low (200°) for 8 to 10 hours. Remove meat and bones from broth. Dice meat and discard bones. Skim fat. Return meat to broth and adjust seasonings. Heat through and ladle into bowls.

HEARTY VEGETABLE VEAL SOUP

Serve with crusty bread, a fruit basket and cheese board for a complete meal.

2 lb. veal shanks
2 qt. water
1 tsp. salt
2 potatoes, peeled and diced
2 carrots, peeled and sliced
1½ cups shredded green cabbage
1 onion, chopped

1 stalk celery, diced
1 can (8 oz.) tomato sauce
freshly ground pepper to taste
½ tsp. dried oregano
½ tsp. dried basil
½ tsp. dried thyme

Place veal, water and salt in the crockery pot. Heat on high (300°) for 2 hours. Remove meat and allow to cool. Discard bones and dice meat. Return to crockery pot. Add remaining ingredients and cook on low (200°) for 3 hours.

MOROCCAN MEATBALL SOUP

Chopped tomatoes freshen this spicy meal-in-one soup.

1/3 cup lentils, with water to cover
1 onion, chopped
1 carrot, peeled and grated
1 stalk celery, chopped
2 tbs. vegetable oil
3/4 cup tomato sauce
1 tsp. grated ginger root, or 1/4 tsp. ground ginger
1/2 tsp. salt
1/2 tsp. ground cumin
dash seasoned pepper
1 1/2 qt. homemade or canned low fat beef or chicken broth
Meatballs, follows
1 large tomato, peeled and chopped
3 tbs. chopped fresh cilantro

Place lentils with water to cover in a saucepan. Cover and bring to a boil; simmer for 45 minutes, or until almost tender. Drain. In a large skillet, sauté onion, carrot and celery in oil until glazed. Transfer to the crockery pot. Add cooked lentils, tomato sauce, ginger, salt, cumin, pepper and broth. Cover and cook on low (200°) for 4 hours, or on high (300°) for 2 hours. Prepare meatballs while lentils are cooking in crockery pot. When lentils are done, drop meatballs into simmering soup. Cover and cook on high for 30 minutes to 1 hour. Add tomato and cilantro and serve steaming hot.

MEATBALLS

1 lb. ground lamb
⅓ cup homemade or canned low fat
  beef or chicken broth
3 tbs. flour

1 tsp. salt
1 clove garlic, minced
2 tbs. chopped fresh cilantro
flour for rolling meatballs

Mix ingredients together and form into ¾-inch balls. Roll in flour and add to soup as directed.

MEXICAN ALBONDIGAS SOUP

Lime juice and cilantro spark this Mexican meatball soup. Accompany with hot rolled tortillas, and finish off the meal with tropical fruit.

1 lb. lean ground beef
2 qt. homemade or canned low fat
  chicken broth
3 tbs. flour
1 egg
1 red chile pepper, seeds removed
4 carrots, peeled and grated

⅓ cup chopped fresh cilantro
3 tbs. long-grain rice
½ lb. spinach, shredded
2 tsp. fresh oregano, or ½ tsp. dried
2 tbs. diced ham
2 limes, cut into wedges

Combine ground meat, ⅓ cup chicken stock, flour and egg. Mix well and shape into 1-inch meatballs. Place remaining chicken broth, chile pepper, carrots, cilantro and rice in the crockery pot. Heat on high (300°). When broth simmers, add meatballs. Cover and cook on high for 30 minutes. Reduce heat to low (200°). Cook for 2 to 3 hours. Add spinach, oregano and ham. Heat until steaming. Ladle into bowls. Pass lime wedges.

FRENCH ONION SOUP

The wines mellow and lend a subtle flair to this aromatic French-style onion soup.

4 large yellow onions, thinly sliced
2 tbs. butter
3 cups homemade or canned low fat beef broth
1 cup dry white wine
1/4 cup medium dry sherry
1 tsp. Worcestershire sauce
1 clove garlic, minced
4-6 slices buttered French bread
1/4 cup grated Romano cheese, or Parmesan cheese

In a large skillet, slowly sauté onions in butter until limp and glazed. Transfer to the crockery pot. Add beef broth, white wine, sherry, Worcestershire sauce and garlic. Cover and cook on low (200°) for 6 to 8 hours. Place French bread on a baking sheet, sprinkle with cheese and place under a preheated broiler until lightly toasted. To serve, ladle soup into bowls. Float a slice of toasted French bread on top of each serving.

COUNTRY-STYLE BEAN SOUP

Servings: 8
Cooking time: 6-8 hours

A meaty ham bone lends substance to a peasant-style pot of bean soup.

1½ cups small white beans, soaked
  overnight, drained
8 cups water
1 large onion, finely chopped
2 carrots, peeled and shredded
1 stalk celery, finely chopped

3 tbs. olive oil
2 cloves garlic, minced
1 bay leaf
1 meaty ham bone, or ham hock
salt and pepper to taste
finely chopped fresh parsley for garnish

Cover beans with 6 cups water and simmer in a saucepan for 1½ hours, or until almost tender. Transfer beans and liquid to the crockery pot. In a large skillet, sauté onion, carrots and celery in oil until limp. Transfer to crockery pot. Add garlic, bay leaf, ham bone, salt, pepper and 2 cups water. Cover and cook on low (200°) for 6 to 8 hours. Ladle into soup bowls and sprinkle with parsley.

GREEK LENTIL SOUP

Hearty bean and lentil soups native to the Middle East and Central Europe are an ideal choice for crockery pot cooking.

1½ cups dried lentils
4½ cups water
1 medium onion, chopped
1 carrot, peeled and grated
1 stalk celery, chopped
3 tbs. olive oil, or vegetable oil
1 bay leaf

2 cloves garlic, minced
salt and pepper to taste
½ tsp. dried oregano
1 beef bouillon cube
½ cup tomato sauce
3 tbs. red wine vinegar

Simmer lentils in water for 45 minutes, or until almost tender. Transfer to the crockery pot. In a large skillet, sauté onion, carrot and celery in oil until limp and glazed. Transfer to crockery pot. Add bay leaf, garlic, salt, pepper, oregano and bouillon cube. Cover and cook on low (200°) for 6 to 8 hours. Add tomato sauce and vinegar and stir well. Cover and cook on high (300°) for 30 minutes, or until flavors are well blended.

SWEDISH-STYLE PEA SOUP

Carrots contribute a pleasant hue and sweetness when smoothly blended into this pea soup. It makes a nourishing luncheon entrée or a warm welcome for famished skiers.

1 cup yellow split peas
1 meaty ham hock
2 qt. water
½ tsp. dry mustard
2-3 carrots, peeled and diced
1 onion, peeled and diced
salt and pepper to taste
2 tbs. dry sherry, optional

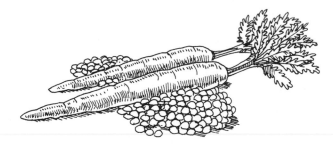

Place peas in the crockery pot with ham hock, water, mustard, carrots and onion. Cover and cook on low (200°) for 8 to 12 hours, or until peas are tender. Remove ham hock and dice meat. Place vegetables and pea broth in a blender container. Cover and blend until smooth. Return to crockery pot. Add diced ham, salt, pepper and sherry, if desired. Heat until steaming.

GREEN SPLIT PEA AND HAM SOUP

Servings: 8
Cooking time: 7-9 hours

This hearty soup makes a perfect midwinter supper. In Sweden it is a traditional Thursday evening entrée.

1½ cups dried green split peas
2 qt. water
1 small onion, chopped
1 stalk celery, chopped
1 bay leaf
1 tbs. chopped fresh parsley

salt and freshly ground pepper
 to taste
1 cup chopped cooked ham
2 medium carrots, shredded
1 tbs. Dijon mustard

Place peas, water, onion, celery, bay leaf, parsley, salt and pepper in the crockery pot. Cover and cook on low (200°) for 6 to 8 hours, or until peas are soft. Add ham, carrots and mustard and cook for 1 hour.

POTAGE MONGOLE

Enrich this classic soup with crabmeat or shrimp for a hearty luncheon or supper soup. Without the seafood, it makes an intriguing starter for a party dinner.

½ tsp. curry powder
1 tsp. butter
1 can (10¾ oz.) tomato soup
1 can (11½ oz.) green pea soup
1 bottle (8 oz.) clam juice
2 cups water
2 tbs. dry sherry
1 cup crabmeat, or shrimp, optional
finely chopped fresh parsley for garnish

Heat the crockery pot to high (300°). Add curry powder and butter and sauté until glazed (this removes the "raw" taste from curry powder). Add soups, clam juice and water. Cover and heat on high (300°). Add sherry and crabmeat. Heat until steaming. Ladle into soup bowls and sprinkle with parsley.

HOT BORSCH

Serve with dark pumpernickel bread to turn this soup into a full meal.

2 lb. beef shanks
1 tsp. salt
½ tsp. pepper
2 cloves garlic, chopped
2 qt. water
4 beets, peeled and shredded
1 onion, chopped
2 cups chopped red or white cabbage

1 carrot, grated
3 tbs. lemon juice
⅓ cup tomato paste
1 lb. Polish sausage
sour cream or yogurt, and chopped
   chives or green onion tops, for
   condiments

Combine beef, salt, pepper, garlic and water in the crockery pot. Cover; cook on high (300°) for 3 hours. Remove meat from crockery pot, allow to cool slightly and pull meat from bones. Add meat, beets, onion, cabbage, carrots, lemon juice and tomato paste to crockery pot. Cook on low (200° for 3 hours. Skim any fat. To serve, brown sausages well on all sides, slice and add to crockery pot. Serve with condiments.

CREAM OF CORN SOUP

This smooth vegetable soup is especially good preceding a roast pork, ham or turkey dinner.

1 can (15 oz.) cream-style corn
2 cups rich chicken stock
1 tbs. chopped celery
1 tbs. chopped onion
1 tsp. Worcestershire sauce

½ tsp. celery salt
2 cups milk
salt and pepper to taste
sour cream and toasted slivered
  almonds for garnish

Combine corn, chicken stock, celery, onion, Worcestershire sauce and celery salt in the crockery pot. Cover and cook on low (200°) for 2 hours. Puree in a blender. Return to crockery pot and add milk, salt and pepper. Heat until steaming. Ladle into soup bowls, and garnish with sour cream and almonds.

FISH AND SHELLFISH

Fish and shellfish are delicate and should always be prepared with care and gentleness. They demand more precise watching and timing than most foods cooked in a crockery pot. If overcooked, they lose their juicy tenderness. The low temperature setting of slow cookers is perfect, but, unlike meat, cooking fish and shellfish for an extra long time is destined to shrink the delicate fibers and make the flesh tough. In timing, be sure to allow for variables that will occur with different-shaped pieces. Feel free to test for doneness before the specified time is up. When fish is done, it will flake easily when tested with a fork but will still be moist. Shellfish requires very little cooking time. Both should be removed from the crockery pot as soon as they are done.

POACHED SALMON

*Poach a large piece of salmon for two meals. Serve part of it warm with **Cilantro Vinaigrette**. This recipe is also used for **Swedish Salmon Plate**, page 30. and **Salmon in Aspic**, page 28.*

2 lb. (or larger) piece salmon
½ cup dry white wine
½ cup water
1 bay leaf
several celery leaves
1 green onion, sliced
½ tsp. salt
1 tbs. lemon juice
½ lemon, thinly sliced
Cilantro Vinaigrette, follows

Place salmon in the crockery pot. Pour in wine and water. Add bay leaf, celery leaves, onion, salt and lemon juice. Lay lemon slices on top of salmon. Cover and cook on low (200°) for 2 to 3 hours, or until salmon flakes when tested with a fork.

Remove salmon from crockery pot. Strain poaching juices into a jar. Cover and chill until needed for *Salmon in Aspic*. Remove skin and bones from salmon. Cut half of salmon into serving pieces. Serve warm with *Cilantro Vinaigrette*. Prepare *Swedish Salmon Plate* or *Salmon in Aspic* with remaining half of fish.

CILANTRO VINAIGRETTE

¼ cup olive oil
3 tbs. lemon juice
1 shallot, or green onion, finely chopped
3 tbs. finely chopped fresh cilantro

    Combine ingredients; serve in a sauce boat.

SALMON IN ASPIC

*With half of the recipe for **Poached Salmon**, page 26, prepare salmon in jellied aspic to make a handsome, French-style first course. Or if you prefer, serve it as an entrée salad, garnished with cherry tomatoes, marinated artichoke hearts and crisp cucumber spears.*

1 cup poaching juices (see *Poached Salmon*)
½ cup dry white wine
1½ tsp. unflavored gelatin
½ cup cold water
3 doz. large capers
1 lb. *Poached Salmon*
½ cup *Yogurt-Sour Cream Dill Sauce*
  for garnish, follows

Remove any solidified fat from the top of jellied poaching juices. Heat juices and wine until steaming. Soften gelatin in cold water and add to hot mixture. Remove from heat and stir until gelatin is dissolved. Pour layer of aspic into 6 small molds or custard cups. (Set remaining aspic mixture aside. Do not chill.) Place 6 capers in each mold. Chill. When set, lay pieces of salmon, bones and skin removed, on each jellied layer.

Pour in remaining aspic to cover. Chill until set. To serve, quickly dip molds into warm water and turn out onto plates. Garnish with *Yogurt-Sour Cream Dill Sauce*.

YOGURT-SOUR CREAM DILL SAUCE

$\frac{1}{2}$ cup yogurt
$\frac{1}{2}$ cup sour cream
2 tbs. minced fresh parsley
$\frac{1}{2}$ tsp. dried dill
1 shallot, chopped
salt and freshly ground pepper to taste

Mix ingredients together until well blended.

SWEDISH SALMON PLATE

Servings: 4

Poached Salmon, page 26, *with a sprightly caper dressing is a refreshing summer supper.*

salad greens
1 lb. cold *Poached Salmon*
1 jar (6 oz.) marinated artichoke hearts
1/3 lb. mushrooms, sliced

3 hard-cooked eggs, sliced
1 cucumber, peeled and sliced
1 cup cherry tomatoes, halved
Caper Dressing, follows

Line a large platter with greens. Place salmon in a chunk in the center. Arrange drained artichoke hearts, sliced mushrooms, eggs, cucumbers and tomatoes around salmon. Serve buffet-style. Pass *Caper Dressing*.

CAPER DRESSING

1/4 cup yogurt
1/4 cup mayonnaise
1 tsp. Dijon mustard
2 tbs. chopped fresh parsley

2 tbs. capers
1/2 tsp. fresh dill
salt and pepper to taste

Mix ingredients together. Makes 1 cup.

GINGERED WHOLE TROUT

Ginger, soy and sherry imbue a whole trout with an Oriental flavor as it steam-cooks in a crockery pot.

1 fresh trout, or red snapper, about
  1½ lb.
1 green onion, white part only, minced
2 tbs. dry sherry
1 tbs. light soy sauce

1 tsp. dark sesame oil
1 tbs. canola oil
1 tbs. minced ginger root
⅓ cup water
fresh cilantro sprigs for garnish

Rinse fish and pat dry. Place in a crockery pot. Mix together onion, sherry, soy sauce, sesame oil, canola oil and ginger. Spoon into fish cavity. Add water. Cover and cook on low (200°) for 1½ hours, or until fish is just firm to the touch. Garnish with cilantro sprigs.

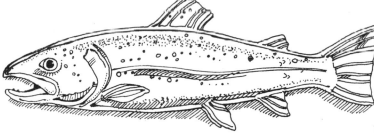

BAKED FISH, PLAKA-STYLE

Servings: 4
Cooking time: 1½ hours

Fish fillets are smothered in vegetables for this flavorful Grecian dish.

4 medium onions, thinly sliced
3 tbs. olive oil
2 tomatoes
½ cup finely chopped fresh parsley
2 cloves garlic, minced

1⅓ lb. turbot or sole fillets
2 tbs. lemon juice
salt and pepper to taste
1 lemon, thinly sliced

In a large skillet, slowly sauté onions in oil until golden brown and almost caramelized. Peel and chop 1 tomato. Add to onions, along with parsley and garlic. Simmer for a few minutes longer. Place fish fillets in a lightly buttered crockery pot. Sprinkle with lemon juice, salt and pepper. Spoon sautéed vegetables over fish. Slice remaining tomato and place on vegetables. Top with lemon slices. Cover and cook on low (200°) for about 1½ hours, or until fish flakes when tested with a fork.

TURBOT IN A CLOAK

The zest of citrus peel permeates fish fillets as they bake to tenderness in this low calorie entrée. You can also use sole or red snapper in this recipe.

1⅓ lb. turbot fillets
1 tsp. butter
salt and pepper to taste
3 green onions, finely chopped
1 tbs. olive oil
½ cup finely chopped fresh parsley
1 tsp. grated lemon peel
1 tsp. grated orange peel
1 orange, thinly sliced, for garnish

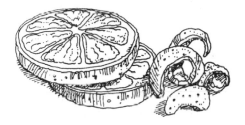

Place fish fillets in a buttered crockery pot. Sprinkle with salt and pepper. Toss onions in oil just to coat. Stir in parsley and citrus peels. Sprinkle over fish. Cover and cook on low (200°) for about 1½ hours, or until fish flakes when tested with a fork. Transfer to a serving platter and arrange an orange slice on top of each fillet.

FISH FILLETS PAPRIKA-STYLE

Sour cream and paprika add a nice Hungarian touch to this fish entrée.

1⅓ lb. sole, turbot or other white fish fillets
salt and pepper to taste
1 tsp. butter
⅔ cup sour cream
2 tsp. flour
3 green onions, finely chopped
3 tbs. dry white wine
½ tsp. paprika (Hungarian-style preferred)
chopped fresh parsley for garnish
lemon wedges for garnish

Season fish fillets with salt and pepper. Butter the crockery pot and insert fish. Mix together sour cream, flour, onions and wine; spoon over fish. Sprinkle fish with paprika. Cover and cook on low (200°) for about 1½ hours, or until fish flakes when tested with a fork. Garnish each serving with parsley and lemon wedges.

SHRIMP-STUFFED SOLE ROLLS

Fish rolls poach to tenderness in a sherried sauce. This easy recipe makes a nice entrée for company without a great deal of work.

6 sole fillets, about 1½ lb.
salt and pepper to taste
2 tbs. plus 1 tsp. butter
½ lb. small cooked shrimp, or 1 can
  (6½ oz.) small shrimp, rinsed and
  drained
⅓ cup pale dry sherry

1 can (10½ oz.) cream of mushroom
  soup, undiluted
2 tbs. lemon juice
¼ cup grated Parmesan cheese
paprika for dusting
fresh parsley for garnish

Season each fish fillet with salt and pepper and dot with 1 tsp. butter. Spoon about 2 tbs. shrimp in center of each fillet and roll up. Skewer with toothpicks. Butter the crockery pot with remaining butter; add fish rolls. Combine sherry, soup and lemon juice and pour over fish. Sprinkle with cheese and dust lightly with paprika. Cover and cook on low (200°) for about 1½ hours, or until fish flakes when tested with a fork. Garnish with parsley.

SCALLOPS IN WINE

Scallops and mushrooms braise together for a succulent sauce to spoon over pilaf.

¼ cup butter
¼ cup dry white wine
2 tbs. minced fresh parsley
1 tbs. chopped shallot, or green onion
2 tbs. pale dry sherry
1 lb. scallops
½ lb. mushrooms, thinly sliced

Combine butter, wine, parsley, shallot and sherry in the crockery pot. Cook, uncovered, on high (300°) until sauce bubbles and is reduced slightly. Add scallops and mushrooms. Cover and cook for 10 to 15 minutes, or until cooked through.

CIOPPINO GENOVESE

In this fun-to-eat fish stew, the shrimp, crab and clams are cooked right in the sauce with their shells still on, so each person must remove his or her own.

1 onion, finely chopped
¼ cup olive oil
2 cloves garlic, minced
2 tbs. chopped fresh parsley
1 can (16 oz.) tomatoes
1 can (8 oz.) tomato sauce
1 tbs. chopped fresh basil, or ¾ tsp. dried

salt and pepper to taste
½ cup pale dry sherry
1 bottle (8 oz.) clam juice
1 lb. rock cod, or halibut
1 doz. (or more) fresh clams
12 medium fresh shrimp
1 fresh cracked crab, uncooked

In a large skillet, sauté onion in oil until glazed. Add garlic and parsley. Sauté for a few minutes and transfer to the crockery pot. Add tomatoes, tomato sauce, basil, salt, pepper, sherry and clam juice. Cover and cook on low (200°) for 2 hours (or on high at 300° for 1 hour). Cut fish into 2-inch cubes. Add fish cubes, clams, shrimp and crab. Cover and cook on high (300°) for 30 minutes, or until shrimp turn pink, clams open and fish flakes when tested with a fork. Ladle into large soup bowls.

POULTRY

Poultry cooked in a crockery pot is remarkably succulent. Since the variety of chicken dishes is endless, and because chicken is plentiful, popular and economical, most of the recipes that follow call for chicken. However, other kinds of poultry, such as turkey parts or game hens, or even rabbit may be used.

LEMON-BASTED TURKEY BREAST

Servings: 8
Cooking time: 6-8 hours

A tangy lemon and herb marinade permeates turkey for a treat to serve hot, or cold in salads and sandwiches.

1 turkey breast, about 2½ lb.

MARINADE

coarsely grated peel and juice of 2 lemons
2 tbs. fresh rosemary, or 1 tsp. dried
2 tbs. fresh oregano, or 1 tsp. dried
2 tbs. Dijon mustard
½ cup white wine
salt and pepper to taste
2 cloves garlic, minced

Place turkey, skin side down, in a nonmetallic dish. Combine marinade ingredients and spoon over, turning to coat turkey. Cover and refrigerate for several hours or overnight. To cook, place turkey and marinade in the crockery pot and cook on low (200°) for 6 to 8 hours, or until tender.

WINE-GLAZED TURKEY DRUMSTICKS

Herb-seasoned turkey drumsticks are excellent hot or cold. It's just as easy to do a double recipe at one time.

2 turkey drumsticks, about 12 oz. each
peel of 1 lemon, cut into matchstick
  strips
1½ tbs. lemon juice
½ cup dry red wine
1 tbs. olive oil

1 tbs. fresh rosemary, or ¼ tsp. dried
2 tbs. chopped fresh parsley
1 shallot, or green onion, chopped
1 clove garlic, minced
salt and pepper to taste
1 lemon, thinly sliced and seeded

Peel skin from turkey pieces. In a bowl, mix together lemon peel, lemon juice, wine, oil, rosemary, parsley, shallot, garlic, salt and pepper. Place turkey pieces in a plastic bag, pour in marinade, seal and refrigerate for at least 4 hours. To cook, place turkey in the crockery pot and add lemon slices. Pour marinade over turkey. Cover and cook on low (200°) for 7 to 8 hours, or on high (300°) for 4 hours, or until tender.

BASQUE CHICKEN AND SAUSAGE

Serve this savory chicken stew in individual ramekins with crusty bread to dip into the juices.

1 onion, chopped
1 carrot, chopped
1 tbs. olive oil
6 chicken thighs
6 mild Italian sausages
6 yellow crookneck squash, sliced
  lengthwise
1 pkg. (10 oz.) baby lima beans, thawed

2 cloves garlic, minced
⅓ cup dry white wine
⅓ cup homemade or canned low fat
  chicken broth
salt and freshly ground pepper
½ tsp. dried tarragon
2 tbs. minced fresh parsley for garnish

In a skillet, sauté onion and carrot in oil until soft. Push to sides of skillet and add chicken; brown on all sides. Transfer to the crockery pot. Add sausages, squash, beans, garlic, wine, broth, salt, pepper and tarragon. Cover and cook on high (300°) for 1½ to 2 hours, or until chicken is cooked through. Sprinkle with parsley.

STUFFED ROAST CHICKEN

Servings: about 6
Cooking time: 7-8 hours

A plump, stuffed chicken is an ideal choice to roast in a crockery pot.

1 whole broiler-fryer chicken, 3 lb.
1½ cups mixed white and wild rice
1 tsp. olive oil or butter
salt and pepper to taste

½ tsp. grated lemon peel
¼ cup golden raisins
½ cup dry white wine

Wash chicken and pat dry. Cook rice according to package directions until barely tender. In a large skillet, brown chicken in oil or butter. Turn to brown on all sides. Season well with salt and pepper. Sprinkle lemon peel inside cavity. Mix raisins into rice mixture and spoon into cavity. Skewer opening closed. Place chicken in the crockery pot and pour in wine. Cover and cook on low (200°) for 7 to 8 hours, or until tender. Transfer chicken to a carving board. Skim fat from crockery pot and pour juices into a sauce boat. Carve bird and serve at once. Pass juice.

LEMON ROAST CHICKEN

Greek cooks season roast chicken in a simple fashion: rubbed with garlic, oregano and lemon juice. The result is a succulent and aromatic dish.

1 whole broiler-fryer chicken,
  3 lb. or larger
salt and pepper to taste
1 tsp. dried oregano

2 cloves garlic, minced
1 tsp. olive oil or butter
¼ cup water
3 tbs. lemon juice ++

Wash chicken. Pat dry with paper towels. Season chicken with salt and pepper. Sprinkle half the oregano and garlic inside cavity. Heat oil or butter in a large skillet. Brown chicken on all sides. Transfer to the crockery pot. Sprinkle with remaining oregano and garlic. Add water to skillet and stir to loosen browned bits. Pour into crockery pot. Cover and cook on low (200°) for 8 hours. Add lemon juice for last hour of cooking. Transfer chicken to a carving board. Skim fat from crockery pot, and pour juices into a sauce boat. Carve bird. Serve with some of juices spooned over chicken.

HAWAIIAN CHICKEN

Servings: 4
Cooking time: 3-4 hours

Pineapple slices and avocado spears complement golden chicken breasts.

4 green onions
1 tbs. olive oil
4 chicken breast halves
flour seasoned with salt and pepper
  to taste

1 can (14¼ oz.) sliced pineapple,
  canned in natural juices
1 avocado, peeled
hot rice

Chop onions using white part and 1 inch of green tops. Sauté in 1 tsp. olive oil until glazed and transfer to the crockery pot. Coat chicken breasts with seasoned flour and sauté in remaining olive oil until brown on both sides. Transfer to crockery pot. Drain pineapple and pour juice over chicken. Cover and cook on low (200°) for 3 to 4 hours, or on high (300°) for 1½ to 2 hours, or until breasts are tender. Slice avocado into 8 lengthwise strips. Place 2 strips on each chicken breast. Serve over hot rice accompanied by pineapple slices.

CHICKEN WITH CALVADOS

Servings: 4-6
Cooking time: 6-8 hours

The Normandy section of France is noted for this tender, juicy chicken entrée.

1 large broiler-fryer chicken, or 4
  breast halves and 4 thighs
2 tsp. olive oil
salt and pepper to taste
¼ cup Calvados
1 tsp. chicken stock base, or 1 bouillon
  cube

2 tbs. chopped fresh parsley
2 tsp. fresh mixed herbs, or ½ tsp. dried
½ cup dry white wine
1 tbs. arrowroot
2 tbs. cold water
¼ cup heavy cream

Wash chicken and cut into serving pieces. Pat dry with paper towels. In a large skillet, sauté chicken in oil until nicely browned. Season with salt and pepper. Pour Calvados over chicken and carefully ignite. Use a long wooden match, if available. Spoon pan juices over chicken while flaming. Remove chicken and juices to crockery pot. Combine chicken stock base, parsley, herbs and wine. Pour over chicken. Cover and cook on low (200°) for 6 to 8 hours. Remove chicken to a heated platter. Turn crockery pot heat to high (300°). Bend arrowroot with water and stir into juices. Cook on high until mixture thickens and boils. Stir in cream. Heat to serving temperature.

COQ AU VIN

no

Chicken takes on a rich smoky flavor and tang of wine in this classic entrée.

3 green onions
3 slices bacon, diced
1 whole broiler-fryer chicken, about 3 lb.
salt and pepper to taste
½ tsp. dried thyme
8 small whole onions
2 cups dry red wine
2 tsp. chicken stock base, or 2 bouillon cubes
1 clove garlic, minced
½ lb. mushrooms
1 tsp. butter
1 tsp. olive oil
1½ tbs. cornstarch
2 tbs. cold water
fresh parsley for garnish

Chop white part only of green onions; sauté with bacon in a large skillet until bacon is crisp. Transfer to the crockery pot. Wash chicken and pat dry with paper towels. Add to bacon drippings. Season with salt, pepper and thyme. Brown on all sides and transfer to crockery pot. Peel whole onions. Cut a small cross in the root end of each. Brown onions in remaining drippings. Add to crockery pot. Pour wine into skillet and stir to loosen browned bits. Add chicken stock base and stir until dissolved. Pour over chicken. Add garlic and cover crockery pot. Cook on low (200°) for 6 to 8 hours. Slice mushrooms; sauté in butter and oil. Add to chicken. Turn heat to high (300°). When juices bubble, stir in cornstarch and water, which have been blended together. Cook until thickened and serve sprinkled with parsley.

CHICKEN PROVENÇAL

This country-style chicken entrée intertwines the influence of Spanish, French and Italian cuisines. Rice pilaf or risotto makes a good side dish.

1 broiler-fryer chicken, about 3 lb.,
  cut into pieces
3 slices bacon, diced
1 tsp. olive oil
1 carrot, peeled and grated
4 shallots, chopped
3 tbs. brandy, or cognac

2 tomatoes, peeled and chopped
2/3 cup dry red wine
1 tsp. fresh marjoram, or 1/2 tsp. dried
1 tsp. fresh tarragon, or 1/4 tsp. dried
1 tsp. fresh basil, or 1/4 tsp. dried
salt and pepper to taste

Wash chicken pieces and pat dry with paper towels. In a large skillet, brown bacon until crisp. Remove from skillet; pour off drippings. Add oil to skillet, and sauté carrot and shallots until limp. Push to sides of skillet. Add chicken pieces and sauté until brown. Pour in brandy and ignite. When flames die, transfer chicken and vegetables to the crockery pot. Add tomatoes, wine, herbs, bacon, salt and pepper. Cover and cook on low (200°) for 8 hours. Remove cover, skim off fat and cook juices down until reduced by half.

POACHED CHICKEN

Makes: 2½-3 cups chicken meat and 1 cup jellied stock
Cooking time: 7-8 hours

Chicken poached in a crockery pot is the best ever. Whenever possible, poach an extra one to use in cool supper salads, crepes, enchiladas and other casseroles. This is a basic poaching method. Cooking time will be the same even when the recipe is doubled. A 4½-quart crockery pot will accommodate two whole 3 lb. chickens nicely.

1 whole broiler-fryer chicken,
  about 3 lb.
salt and pepper to taste
one 2-inch piece celery
1 carrot

½ medium onion
1 cup homemade or canned low fat
  chicken broth
1 bay leaf

Wash chicken. Pat dry with paper towels and place in the crockery pot. Season with salt and pepper. Tuck celery, carrot and onion around chicken. Pour in broth and add bay leaf. Cover and cook on low (200°) for 7 to 8 hours, or until chicken is tender. Lift chicken from crockery pot. Allow to stand until cool enough to handle. Strain broth into a container. Chill; remove fat before using. Remove chicken meat from bones in pieces as large as possible. Place in a container, cover and chill.

POACHED CHICKEN VÉRONIQUE

Servings: 6
Cooking time: 7-8 hours

Seedless grapes add a special flavor to chicken. If you use chicken parts instead, cooking time will be reduced by about 1 hour.

1 whole broiler-fryer chicken, 3-3½ lb.
1 tsp. olive oil
1 small carrot, peeled and chopped
1 small onion, chopped
½ cup homemade or canned low fat
  chicken broth

½ cup dry white wine
salt and pepper to taste
3 tbs. orange marmalade
1 tbs. lemon juice
1½ cups red or green seedless grapes

Wash chicken. Pat dry with paper towels. In a large skillet, brown chicken in oil. Add carrot and onion. Sauté until glazed. Transfer chicken and vegetables to the crockery pot. Pour broth and wine into skillet and stir to loosen browned bits. Pour over chicken and season with salt and pepper. Cover and cook on low (200°) for 7 to 8 hours, or until tender. Transfer chicken to a heated platter and keep warm. Strain juices into a saucepan. Discard cooking vegetables. Skim fat from juices and bring to a boil. Cook until reduced to 1 cup. Add marmalade, lemon juice and grapes. Heat to serving temperature and serve in a sauce boat. Pass with chicken.

POACHED CHICKEN IN TARRAGON WINE SAUCE

Servings: 4-6
Cooking time: 8 hours

An herb-flavored wine sauce gilds this roasted bird.

1 whole broiler-fryer chicken, 3-3½ lb.
1 carrot, peeled and chopped
1 onion, chopped
1 tsp. olive oil
1 bay leaf

1 cup dry white wine
1 cup chicken stock
2 tsp. fresh tarragon, or ½ tsp. dried
salt and pepper to taste

Wash chicken and pat dry with paper towels. Sauté carrot and onion in oil in a large skillet; transfer to the crockery pot. Brown chicken in remaining drippings; transfer to crockery pot. Add remaining ingredients. Cover and cook on low (200°) for 8 hours. Remove chicken and keep warm. Pour juices into a saucepan and skim fat. Bring to a boil. Cook until reduced to 1 cup. Pour into a sauce boat. Carve chicken and serve. Pass sauce.

VARIATION

Beat 2 egg yolks with ⅓ cup heavy cream. Stir part of reduced sauce into cream mixture. Return to saucepan. Cook, stirring, until thickened. Pass with chicken.

CHINESE SHREDDED CHICKEN SALAD

Shop in an Oriental market for the specialty ingredients you need for this intriguing tossed chicken salad — or you may find them in the Oriental section of some well-stocked markets. Rice sticks are translucent noodles. Directions for **Poached Chicken** *are on page 49.*

1 large chicken breast, 8-10 oz.,
  poached
1 small head iceberg lettuce, shredded
3 green onions, thinly sliced
1 small bunch fresh cilantro
1 stalk celery, thinly sliced

oil for sautéing rice sticks
2 oz. Oriental rice sticks
Sesame Oil Dressing, follows
1/4 cup toasted sesame seeds
1 avocado

Shred chicken and combine with lettuce, onions, cilantro sprigs and celery in a large salad bowl. Cover and chill while preparing other ingredients. Heat about 1/2-inch oil in a large skillet. Add one small handful of rice sticks at a time and sauté just until puffed. Lift out with a slotted spoon and drain on paper towels. The noodles cook quickly, so it is easier to work with small amounts. When ready to serve salad, add noodles to chilled salad ingredients. Pour *Sesame Oil Dressing* over salad and toss lightly. Sprinkle with sesame seeds. Peel and slice avocado and arrange in a pinwheel on top.

SESAME OIL DRESSING

1/2 tsp. salt
1/2 tsp. pepper
3 tbs. white wine vinegar
2 tbs. brown sugar, firmly packed
1/4 cup canola oil
1 1/2 tbs. sesame oil

In a small container, mix ingredients together. Makes about 1/2 cup.

KEN IN ORANGE SAUCE

...ge juice concentrate and currant jelly make a piquant, delicious sauce.

1 broiler-fryer chicken, 3-3½ lb.,
  cut into pieces
1 tsp. olive oil
1 carrot, peeled and chopped
1 green onion, chopped
1 cup homemade or canned low fat
  chicken broth

salt and pepper to taste
¼ cup frozen orange juice concentrate,
  thawed
¼ cup currant jelly
1 orange, peeled and cut into
  segments, for garnish
1 bunch watercress for garnish, optional

Wash chicken and pat dry with paper towels. In a large skillet, brown chicken in oil. Add carrot and onion and sauté until glazed. Transfer chicken and vegetables to the crockery pot. Pour broth into skillet and stir to loosen browned bits. Pour over chicken and sprinkle with salt and pepper. Cover and cook on low (200°) for 6 to 8 hours. Remove chicken from crockery pot and keep warm. Strain juices into a saucepan. Skim fat, bring to a boil and cook until reduced to 1 cup. Add orange juice concentrate and currant jelly. Heat until blended. Spoon some of sauce over chicken. Garnish with orange segments and watercress sprigs. Pass remaining sauce.

CHICKEN IN THE POT

Cooking tin

Cook pan juices down to gain a rich, thick sauce for the chicken.

1 whole broiler-fryer chicken, 3½ lb.
salt and pepper to taste
1 tsp. olive oil
water for rinsing chicken
2 carrots, sliced diagonally
2 parsnips, cut into strips
2 stalks celery, cut into 1-inch pieces

1 leek, or 3 green onions, sliced
2 cloves garlic, minced
2 tsp. fresh oregano leaves
2 cups homemade or canned low fat
  chicken broth
1 cup dry white wine

Wash chicken and pat dry with paper towels. Season with salt and pepper. In a large skillet, brown chicken in oil. Transfer to the crockery pot. Rinse out drippings with water and pour into crockery pot. Place carrots, parsnips, celery and leek around chicken. Season vegetables with salt and pepper. Add garlic, oregano, broth and wine. Cover crockery pot and cook on low (200°) for 8 hours, or until tender. Remove chicken and vegetables to a platter. Keep warm. Pour juices into a saucepan, skim fat, bring to a boil and cook until reduced to 1 cup.

CHICKEN CURRY

Servings: 6-8
Cooking time: 7-8 hours

This is a good dish to prepare in stages. Cook the chicken one day and finish it in the sauce the next. Apple chunks add tang and texture to the sauce.

1 whole broiler-fryer chicken, 2½-3 lb.
2 cups water
3 chicken bouillon cubes, or 1 tbs.
  chicken stock base
1 large tart cooking apple
3 tbs. olive oil
1 large onion, finely chopped
3 stalks celery, thinly sliced

1 tbs. curry powder
salt to taste
dash hot red pepper flakes
hot steamed rice
toasted slivered almonds, chutney,
  shelled pistachios, minced chives,
  toasted coconut and golden raisins
  for condiments

Place chicken in the crockery pot with water and bouillon cubes. Cover and cook on low (200°) for 7 to 8 hours, or on high (300°) for 3 to 4 hours, or until tender. Remove from broth; cool. Remove chicken from bones and dice. Peel, core and dice apple. Sauté in oil with onion, celery and curry powder until limp and glazed. Season with salt and pepper flakes. Transfer to crockery pot. Add diced chicken and enough broth to moisten. Cook on low (200°) until hot; serve over rice. Pass condiments.

MEATS

Meats are the real stars of crockery pot cooking. Long, slow cooking at a low temperature results in juicy meats with almost no shrinkage. It is easy to get good results with less expensive cuts of meats, which adds still more to the economy of slow cooking.

Another greatly appreciated feature of crockery pot cooking is the ease with which meat can be kept at a perfect serving temperature without overcooking it.

The recipes offered here include a collection of international dishes, such as French beef stews, German pot roasts, Indian curries, Moroccan tajines, fruited pork chops and country-style patés. All are easily and perfectly prepared this convenient way.

OSSO BUCO

The Milanese receive credit for this renowned veal shank entrée. Crusty bread and risotto are choice partners for absorbing the flavorful juices.

6 veal shanks, 2 inches thick
flour for dusting veal
1 tsp. olive oil
salt and freshly ground pepper to taste
1 onion, chopped
1 carrot, grated
1/2 cup vermouth, or dry white wine

1/2 cup chicken broth
1/3 cup tomato sauce
1 clove garlic, minced
2 tsp. grated lemon peel
2 tbs. minced fresh parsley
1 lemon, thinly sliced, for garnish

Dust veal shanks with flour and shake off excess. In a skillet, heat oil and brown shanks well on all sides. Season with salt and pepper. Transfer to a crockery pot. Add onion and carrot to skillet and sauté until soft. Add vermouth, broth, tomato sauce and garlic. Bring to a boil and pour over shanks. Cover and cook on low (200°) for 8 hours, or until tender. Mix lemon peel and parsley and sprinkle over meat. Garnish with lemon slices.

SAUERBRATEN

In order for the meat to acquire the distinguishing piquancy of this classic German dish, it should be marinated for at least 3 days.

4-5 lb. beef rump roast
Marinade, follows
1 tsp. bacon drippings, or olive oil
1 onion, chopped

1 cup homemade or canned low fat
 beef broth
2 tbs. cornstarch
2 tbs. cold water

Place meat in a deep bowl. Add marinade, cover and refrigerate for at least 3 days. Turn occasionally. To cook, remove meat from marinade. Pat dry with paper towels. Strain marinade and set aside. Heat bacon drippings in a large skillet. Brown meat on all sides. Add onion and sauté until golden. Transfer meat and onion to the crockery pot. Add broth and 1 cup strained marinade. Cover and cook on low (200°) for 8 to 10 hours, or until tender. Remove to a heated platter and keep warm. Turn crockery pot heat to high (300°). Blend cornstarch and water. When gravy is bubbling, stir in cornstarch mixture and cook until thickened. Serve with meat.

MARINADE

1½ cups dry red wine
¾ cup red wine vinegar
1 cup water
1 carrot, peeled and chopped
1 onion, chopped
1 bay leaf
10 whole peppercorns
6 whole cloves
½ tsp. dried thyme
salt and pepper to taste

Combine ingredients in a large saucepan. Bring to a boil, reduce heat and simmer for 5 minutes. Remove from heat, cool and use as directed.

LA MODE

...owned French pot roast is superb when slowly cooked in a crockery pot.

...rump roast
...e, follows
1 tsp. ...ive oil
1 tsp. sesame oil
1 cup water
2 beef bouillon cubes
1/4 cup tomato sauce
chopped fresh parsley for garnish

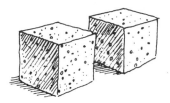

Place roast in a large bowl with marinade. Cover and marinate for 1 day in the refrigerator. Turn occasionally. To cook, remove meat from marinade. Pat dry with paper towels. Heat oils in a large skillet and brown meat on all sides. Transfer to the crockery pot. Strain marinade, reserving vegetables. Add marinade to meat. Sauté vegetables in skillet until glazed and add to meat. Loosen pan drippings with water and add to crockery pot with bouillon and tomato sauce. Cover and cook on low (200°) for 8 hours, or until meat is tender. Transfer meat to a carving board. Pour juices into a saucepan and boil until reduced to 2 cups. Pour juices into a sauce boat, garnish with parsley and serve with meat.

MARINADE

½ tsp. salt
2 tsp. fresh thyme, or ½ tsp. dried
freshly ground pepper to taste
1 carrot, peeled and chopped
1 stalk celery, chopped
1 onion, chopped
2 cloves garlic, minced
2 cups dry red wine

Combine ingredients in a large bowl and use as directed.

GREEK ISLAND VEAL AND POTATOES

Servings: 6
Cooking time: 6-8 hours

A canopied outdoor taverna in the charming Cretan resort of Aghios Nikolai offers this tantalizing stew in fat clay pots. The recipe transfers admirably to a crockery pot.

1 large onion, chopped
1 tsp. olive oil
2 lb. boneless veal stew meat, cut into
 1½-inch cubes
6 small potatoes
3 carrots, cut into ½-inch chunks
4 whole cloves
1 whole cinnamon stick

4 cloves garlic, minced
salt and freshly ground pepper to taste
1½ cups homemade or canned low fat
 chicken broth
3 tbs. tomato paste
¼ cup white wine vinegar
½ cup grated Romano cheese, or
 Parmesan cheese, for garnish

In a large skillet, sauté onion in oil for a few minutes, add meat and cook until browned on all sides. Transfer to a crockery pot with potatoes and carrots. Place whole cloves and cinnamon stick in a tea ball or tie in a cheesecloth bag and add to meat. Add garlic, salt, pepper, broth, tomato paste and vinegar. Stir to blend. Cover and cook on low (200°) for 6 to 8 hours, or until meat is tender. Remove spices. Sprinkle with cheese.

POT ROAST PACIFIC

Teriyaki seasonings richly flavor and glaze this chuck roast.

4-5 lb. chuck roast
1 tbs. olive oil
4 cloves garlic, minced
1 cup dry sherry
⅓ cup soy sauce

1 tbs. minced ginger root, or 1
  ground ginger
freshly ground pepper to taste
2 green onions, thinly sliced
4 whole cloves

Rub roast with oil and minced garlic. Place meat in a glass or stainless steel bowl. Add sherry, soy sauce, ginger, pepper, onions and cloves. Turn meat to coat. Cover and refrigerate overnight. To cook, remove meat from marinade; set marinade aside. Transfer meat to the crockery pot. Add ½ cup reserved marinade. Cover and cook on low (200°) for 7 to 8 hours, or until fork-tender. Transfer to a platter and keep warm. Add ½ cup more marinade to pan juices. Cook down until reduced and pour into a sauce boat. Serve with meat.

GINGERED ROUND STEAK

Fresh ginger root and soy sauce permeate round steak, creating a mahogany glaze.

2 lb. round steak
2 inner stalks celery
4 green onions, chopped
1 tbs. olive oil

3 tbs. soy sauce
⅓ cup red wine
1 tsp. grated ginger root
¼ lb. fresh mushrooms

Cut steak into serving-sized pieces. Slice celery diagonally into 1-inch pieces. In a large skillet, sauté celery and onions in olive oil just until glazed. Remove from skillet and set aside. In the same skillet, brown meat on both sides. Transfer to the crockery pot. Add soy sauce and wine to skillet and stir to loosen browned bits. Pour over meat and sprinkle with ginger. Arrange sautéed vegetables on top. Cover and cook on low (200°) for 6 to 8 hours. Wash and slice mushrooms. Sauté in remaining oil and add to meat during last half hour of cooking.

SAVORY SWISS STEAK

Servings: 6
Cooking time: 6-8 hours

Vegetables thicken the rich sauce, which smothers fork-tender steak.

1½ lb. round steak
¼ cup flour
2 tsp. dry mustard
salt and pepper to taste
1 tsp. olive oil
1 onion, finely chopped

2 carrots, peeled and grated
2 stalks celery, finely chopped
1 can (16 oz.) tomatoes
2 tbs. Worcestershire sauce
2 tsp. brown sugar, firmly packed
chopped fresh parsley for garnish

Cut steak into 6 serving-sized pieces. Coat with mixture of flour, mustard, salt and pepper. In a large skillet, brown meat in oil. Transfer to the crockery pot. In the same skillet, sauté onion, carrots and celery until glazed. Add tomatoes, Worcestershire sauce and brown sugar. Heat, scraping up browned bits, and pour over meat. Cover and cook on low (200°) for 6 to 8 hours, or until tender. To serve, spoon sauce over meat. Sprinkle with parsley.

BEEF IN WALNUT SAUCE

Servings: 12
Cooking time: 8-10 hours

This unusual recipe for spiced beef in a nut sauce, called Lagoto, comes from Greece.

4 lb. rump roast, cut into cubes
seasoned flour for dredging meat
1 tsp. olive oil
½ cup water
1 can (8 oz.) tomato sauce
4-6 cloves garlic, minced
⅓ cup apple cider vinegar

1 whole cinnamon stick
8 whole cloves
8 whole allspice
1 cup ground walnuts
1 tbs. lemon juice
sliced sourdough French bread, toasted
  and buttered

Dredge meat in seasoned flour and shake off excess. In a large skillet, heat oil and brown meat well. Transfer to the crockery pot. Pour water into skillet to loosen browned bits. Add to crockery pot with tomato sauce, garlic and vinegar. Place cinnamon stick, cloves and allspice in a tea ball or cheesecloth bag and add to crockery pot. Cover and cook on low (200°) for 8 to 10 hours, or until very tender. If necessary, cook down pan juices. Add walnuts and lemon juice and heat to serving temperature. Serve beef in sauce over hot buttered French bread toast.

BEEF STIFADO

Pickling spices and red wine vinegar punctuate this Greek stew.

2½ lb. lean stew beef
1 tsp. olive oil
1 can (1 lb.) small onions, drained
1 tbs. brown sugar, firmly packed
½ cup dry red wine
½ cup water
3 tbs. tomato paste

¼ cup red wine vinegar
1 tsp. mixed pickling spices
4 whole cloves
3 cloves garlic, minced
salt and pepper to taste
1 pkg. (12 oz.) frozen petite peas

Cut meat into 1-inch chunks. In a large skillet, heat oil and brown meat. Transfer to the crockery pot. Cook onions and brown sugar in skillet over medium high heat, stirring, until glazed. Transfer to crockery pot. Add wine, water, tomato paste and vinegar to skillet and stir to loosen browned bits. Pour over meat and onions. Place pickling spices and cloves in a tea ball or tie in a cheesecloth bag and add to crockery pot. Season with garlic, salt and pepper. Cover and cook on low (200°) for 8 hours. Thaw peas and add to crockery pot during last half hour of cooking. Cook down juices until slightly reduced. Serve in ramekins.

BEEF EN DAUBE

This traditional French stew is hearty and full of flavor.

2 lb. lean stew beef
2 slices bacon, diced
2 doz. tiny boiling onions
1 tbs. red wine vinegar
1 tbs. brown sugar, firmly packed
1½ cups dry red wine
salt and pepper to taste
2 cloves garlic, minced

1 tsp. fresh thyme, or ½ tsp. dried
1 tsp. beef stock base, or 1 bouillon
  cube
2 strips orange peel
2 tbs. cornstarch
2 tbs. cold water
2 tbs. chopped fresh parsley for garnish

Cut meat into 1-inch cubes. In a large skillet, sauté bacon until crisp. Remove from skillet and set aside. Discard all but 2 tbs. drippings. Brown meat and onions in drippings and transfer to the crockery pot with bacon. Add vinegar and brown sugar to skillet. Cook for 1 minute, stirring. Pour in wine and bring to a boil. Pour over meat. Season with salt, pepper, garlic, thyme, beef stock base and orange peel. Cover and cook on low (200°) for 8 hours. Turn to high (300°). Mix cornstarch with cold water. When pan juices are bubbling, stir in cornstarch mixture. Cook, stirring, until thickened. Garnish with parsley.

CORNED BEEF AND VEGETABLES

Plan two appearances for corned beef. First, serve it hot with vegetables. For the second showing, make delicious Reuben-style sandwiches. Spread slices of rye bread with creamy Russian dressing and layer with corned beef, Swiss cheese and sauerkraut. Grill in butter until the cheese melts.

4 lb. corned beef brisket
3 carrots, cut into 3-inch pieces
2 stalks celery, cut into 2-inch pieces
2 medium onions, quartered
1 cup dry white wine
1 bay leaf
3 whole cloves

Wash brisket under cold running water to remove excess brine. Place in the crockery pot. Add vegetables to crockery pot with wine, bay leaf and cloves. Cover and cook on low (200°) for 8 hours, or until tender. Transfer meat and vegetables to a heated platter. Pour juices into a sauce boat. Serve with meat.

SHORT RIBS PACIFIC-STYLE

A soy sauce glaze penetrates the short ribs as they braise in the crockery pot.

3-4 lb. beef short ribs, cut into
  2- or 3-inch lengths
1 onion, chopped
1 tsp. olive oil
⅔ cup ketchup
3 tbs. soy sauce
2 tbs. apple cider vinegar
2 tbs. brown sugar, firmly packed

Place short ribs on a broiler pan and broil until well browned to remove excess fat. Transfer to the crockery pot. Sauté onion in oil until limp and golden. Add ketchup, soy sauce, vinegar and brown sugar and heat until blended. Pour over ribs. Cover and cook on low (200°) for 8 hours.

GREEK-STYLE MEAT SAUCE

This meat sauce is great for various dishes: spaghetti, moussaka and the Greek macaroni dish, pastitsio. It is also good spooned over tacos or ladled inside avocado half-shells. This recipe makes a large quantity and freezes well.

2 lb. ground turkey, or lean ground beef
1 tsp. olive oil
4 medium onions, finely chopped
4 cans (6 oz. each) tomato paste
4 cloves garlic, minced

1 tsp. mixed pickling spices
1 cup dry red wine
1 tsp. salt
freshly ground pepper to taste

In a large skillet, brown meat in oil until it loses its pink color. Transfer to the crockery pot. In the same skillet, sauté onions until glazed and transfer to crockery pot. Add tomato paste, garlic, pickling spices (placed in a tea ball or tied in a cheesecloth bag), wine, salt and pepper. Cover. Cook on low (200°) for 8 hours. Stir once or twice. Cool slightly. Serve hot or ladle into freezer containers.

GREEK PITAS

A spicy meat sauce to tuck into pita bread pockets provides the centerpiece for a party supper buffet. Ring the crockery pot with a basket of bread and small bowls of condiments. If desired, wrap the breads in foil and heat in the oven before serving.

1½ qt. *Greek-Style Meat Sauce*, page 73
1 cup freshly grated Parmesan cheese, or Romano cheese
½ cup pine nuts, or coarsely chopped pistachios
8 pita breads
3 Roma tomatoes, sliced
4 green onions, chopped
2 avocados, diced

In the crockery pot, combine meat sauce, cheese and nuts. Heat on low (200°) for 1 hour, or until heated through. Split breads in half and place in a basket. To serve, arrange bread and bowls of tomatoes, onions and avocado buffet-style alongside crockery pot. Allow guests to assemble their own sandwiches.

GLAZED SAUSAGE-STRIPED MEAT LOAF

Servings:
Cooking time: 7 hours

Potatoes cut French fry-style bake around this juicy meat loaf.

3 mild Italian sausages, about ¾ lb.
2 eggs
½ cup milk
2 slices bread
1 tsp. salt
1 tsp. Worcestershire sauce
1 tsp. dry mustard
1 tsp. beef stock base

1 small onion, cut into pieces
1½ lb. ground beef chuck
¼ cup ketchup
1 tsp. Dijon mustard
1½ tbs. brown sugar, firmly packed
4 large boiling potatoes
2 tsp. olive oil

In a saucepan, cover sausages with water and simmer for 10 minutes. Drain. Place eggs, milk, bread, salt, Worcestershire sauce, dry mustard, beef stock base and onion in a blender container; blend until smooth. Place ground meat in a mixing bowl. Pour in contents of blender container and mix until smooth. Pat half of meat loaf mixture in the bottom of the crockery pot. Cover with sausages. Top with remaining meat loaf mixture. Pat to seal. Combine ketchup, mustard and brown sugar. Spread over meat. Peel potatoes and cut into strips. Coat well with olive oil and place around meat. Cover and cook on high (300°) for 1 hour. Reduce to low (200°) and cook for 6 hours.

NTINE MEATBALLS

h-flavored meat balls are delicious cooked in a red wine sauce.

1 pkg. (10 oz.) frozen chopped spinach
3 eggs
2 slices fresh bread
2 tbs. minced fresh parsley
¼ cup grated Parmesan cheese
salt and pepper to taste
1 clove garlic, minced
¾ lb. ground beef chuck
¾ lb. ground turkey
1 small onion, grated
flour to coat meatballs
1 tbs. olive oil
Red Wine Sauce, follows

Defrost spinach and squeeze dry. Beat eggs. Mix in bread, parsley, cheese, salt, pepper and garlic. Add meats, spinach and onion. Mix thoroughly to blend. Shape into 1-inch balls. Roll in flour and brown in olive oil in a large skillet. Reserve pan drippings for *Red Wine Sauce*. Transfer to the crockery pot. Pour in *Red Wine Sauce*, cover and cook on low (200°) for 1 to 2 hours.

RED WINE SAUCE

½ cup homemade or canned low fat beef broth
½ cup dry red wine
½ tsp. dried oregano

In the same skillet in which meatballs were browned, add broth and wine to pan drippings and stir. Boil until reduced to ⅓ cup. Add oregano and simmer for a few minutes.

SCANDINAVIAN MEATBALLS

These meatballs are delicious topped with sour cream or yogurt. Leftovers make fine sandwiches; simply split and put between slices of buttered rye bread. Serve with dill pickles.

1 lb. ground pork
1 lb. ground veal, or lean ground beef
¼ cup instant onion soup mix
2 eggs
½ cup quick-cooking oatmeal
⅔ cup milk
2 tbs. chopped fresh parsley
salt and pepper to taste

2 tsp. beef stock base, or 2 bouillon
  cubes
¼ tsp. ground nutmeg
¼ tsp. ground allspice
½ cup homemade or canned low fat
  beef broth
sour cream or yogurt

Place ground meats, onion soup mix, eggs, oatmeal, milk, parsley, salt, pepper, beef stock base, nutmeg and allspice in a mixing bowl. Mix until blended. Shape into 1¼-inch balls. Place 1 inch apart in a shallow baking pan. Bake in a 425° oven for 15 minutes, or until browned. Transfer to the crockery pot. Pour in broth and cover. Cook on low (200°) for 1 to 2 hours. Serve with sour cream or yogurt.

MEATBALLS STROGANOFF

Toasted French bread slices make a great base for this creamy meatball dish.

2 tsp. olive oil
1 medium onion, finely chopped
1 lb. lean ground beef
1 lb. ground turkey
salt and pepper to taste
¼ tsp. dried tarragon
¼ tsp. dried basil
2 tbs. flour
⅓ cup tomato paste

¾ cup homemade or canned low fat
 beef broth
2 tsp. Worcestershire sauce
2 tsp. apple cider vinegar
½ lb. mushrooms, sliced
1 cup (½ pt.) sour cream
sliced French bread, toasted and
 buttered

Heat 1 tsp. olive oil in a large skillet. Sauté onion until golden and transfer to the crockery pot. Quickly shape meat into bite-sized balls. Drop into skillet and sauté, shaking to turn, until browned. Sprinkle with salt, pepper, tarragon, basil and flour. Cook for a few minutes. Transfer to crockery pot. Add tomato paste, broth, Worcestershire sauce and vinegar to skillet. Stir to loosen browned bits. Pour into crockery pot. Cover and cook on high (300°) for 1½ to 2 hours. Sauté mushrooms in remaining olive oil. Add to crockery pot along with sour cream. Heat thoroughly. Serve over French bread.

CALIFORNIA TOSTADAS

Tortillas pyramided with meat sauce and condiments are especially fun for a teenage gathering. The meat sauce freezes well so it can be made ahead.

MEAT SAUCE

2 onions, chopped
1 tsp. olive oil
2 lb. lean ground beef or turkey
salt and pepper to taste
2 cloves garlic, minced
1/2 tsp. ground cumin
1/2 tsp. dried oregano

1/2 tsp. seasoned pepper
1 can (6 oz.) tomato paste
1/2 cup homemade or canned low fat
  beef broth
1 tbs. red wine vinegar
2 tsp. brown sugar, firmly packed

In a large skillet, sauté onions in oil until golden. Transfer to the crockery pot. Brown ground beef in skillet and transfer to crockery pot (use a slotted spoon to lift meat into crockery pot so excess fat will be drained away). Season meat with salt, pepper, garlic, cumin, oregano and seasoned pepper. Add tomato paste, broth, vinegar and brown sugar. Cover and cook on low (200°) for 4 to 6 hours.

vegetable oil for sautéing tortillas
12 tortillas
hot refried beans, shredded lettuce,
  shredded cheddar cheese, chopped
  tomatoes and sliced avocado for condiments

Just before serving time, heat ¼-inch oil in a large skillet. Sauté tortillas, one at a time, for about 30 seconds on each side, or until slightly browned and crisp. Use tongs to handle hot tortillas. Drain on paper towels. Wrap loosely in foil and keep warm in a low oven. Arrange condiments in bowls, arrange tortillas in a basket and serve *Meat Sauce* from crockery pot. Allow guests to assemble their own tostadas by spooning refried beans onto tortillas first, followed by *Meat Sauce*, lettuce and remaining condiments.

VEAL AND APRICOTS TAJINE

The exotic influence of Morocco is evident in this spicy stew.

2 lb. veal stew meat
1 tsp. olive oil
1 medium onion, finely chopped
2 tsp. minced ginger root
1½ tsp. salt
1 tsp. ground cumin
¼ tsp. pepper

1 whole cinnamon stick
2 cloves garlic, minced
¾ cup moist dried apricots
¼ cup golden raisins
1 tbs. honey
1 tbs. lemon juice
¼ cup pine nuts for garnish, optional

Cut veal into 1¼-inch cubes. Heat oil in a large skillet and sauté onion with ginger, salt, cumin, pepper and cinnamon until glazed and golden brown. Add garlic and meat. Brown well. Transfer to the crockery pot. Add apricots and raisins. Cover and cook on low (200°) for 7 to 8 hours, or until meat is tender. Add honey and lemon juice. Turn heat to high (300°). Cook for a few minutes longer. Garnish with pine nuts.

VEAL STEW WITH ONIONS

Mixed pickling spices lend a novel touch to this Greek veal stew.

2 lb. veal stew meat
seasoned flour for rolling meat
1 tsp. olive oil
¼ cup water
3 cloves garlic, minced
½ cup tomato sauce
2 tbs. red wine vinegar
½ tsp. whole mixed pickling spices
1 can (15 oz.) small whole onions, drained
3 tbs. chopped fresh parsley for garnish

Cut meat into 1¼-inch cubes. Roll in flour. Heat oil in a large skillet and brown meat. Transfer to the crockery pot. Add water to skillet and stir to loosen browned bits. Pour into crockery pot. Add garlic, tomato sauce, vinegar and pickling spices (placed in a tea ball or tied in a cheesecloth bag). Cover and cook on low (200°) for 6 to 8 hours. Add onions; heat to serving temperature. Sprinkle with parsley.

TARRAGON VEAL STEW

even better the 2nd day

Servings: 6
Cooking time: 8 hours

Serve this wine-laced stew on a bed of pilaf. Garnish with toasted almonds.

2 lb. veal stew meat
flour seasoned with salt and pepper
  to taste
1 tbs. olive oil
1 cup dry white wine
1 cup beef broth

2 shallots, chopped
2 cloves garlic, minced
1 tsp. dried tarragon
1 ½ tsp. grated lemon peel
2 tbs. heavy cream
1 tsp. lemon juice

Dust veal with seasoned flour. In a large skillet, sauté veal in oil. Transfer to the crockery pot. Pour wine and broth into skillet and stir to loosen browned bits. Pour over veal. Add shallots, garlic, tarragon and lemon peel. Cover and cook on low (200°) for 8 hours. Ladle pan juices into a saucepan. Boil down until reduced and slightly thickened. Stir in cream and lemon juice. Heat, stirring, until blended. Return to crockery pot and heat thoroughly.

MOROCCAN LAMB CHOPS AND PRUNES

Fresh cilantro and ginger root are essential to the authenticity of this aromatic North African entrée.

1 medium onion, finely chopped
1 tsp. olive oil
4 shoulder lamb chops
salt and pepper to taste
1½ tsp. minced ginger root
½ tsp. ground cumin
2 cloves garlic, minced

1 whole cinnamon stick
2 tbs. water
1 tbs. chopped fresh cilantro
1 cup pitted prunes
2 tbs. honey
1½ tbs. lime juice
2 tbs. toasted sesame seeds

In a large skillet, sauté onion in oil until limp. Push to sides of skillet. Brown lamb chops well on both sides. Season with salt and pepper. Add ginger, cumin, garlic and cinnamon stick. Sauté for 1 minute. Transfer to the crockery pot. Add water to skillet and stir to loosen browned bits. Add to crockery pot. Scatter cilantro and prunes over lamb chops. Cover and cook on low (200°) for 6 hours. Stir in honey and lime juice. Heat to serving temperature. Sprinkle with sesame seeds.

BURGUNDY LAMB SHANKS

eve curies likes too

Wine and vegetables produce a robust sauce for slow-cooked shanks.

4 lamb shanks, about 3½ lb. *for 3 of us*
salt and pepper to taste
½ tsp. grated lemon peel
½ tsp. dried oregano
2 cloves garlic, minced
2 tbs. chopped fresh parsley

1 carrot, peeled and chopped
1 onion, chopped
1 tsp. olive oil
1 cup dry red wine
1 beef bouillon cube, or 1 tsp. beef
  stock base *or chicken*

Season shanks with salt, pepper, lemon peel and oregano. Place in the crockery pot and sprinkle with garlic and parsley. In a skillet, sauté carrot and onion in oil and transfer to crockery pot. Pour wine into skillet and add bouillon. Stir to loosen browned bits. Pour over shanks. Cover and cook on low (200°) for 8 hours. If desired, drain juice into a saucepan and boil to reduce and thicken slightly.

TURKISH LAMB AND PINE NUT BALLS

For a Middle Eastern dinner, serve these nut-studded meatballs with hot Arabic bread, cucumber and yogurt salad, pilaf and steamed zucchini.

1½ lb. lean ground lamb
½ cup hot or cold mashed potatoes
1 egg
⅓ cup pine nuts
3 tbs. dried currants
2 tbs. minced fresh parsley
¼ tsp. ground allspice

2 cloves garlic, minced
salt and pepper to taste
1 tsp. vegetable oil
1 medium onion, chopped
1 can (8 oz.) tomato sauce
¼ cup dry red wine

Mix lamb, potatoes, egg, nuts, currants, parsley, allspice, garlic, salt and pepper together well. Shape into 1¼-inch balls. Heat in oil in a large skillet. Brown meatballs on all sides and transfer to the crockery pot. Add onion to skillet and sauté until limp and glazed. Add tomato sauce and wine. Bring to a boil and pour over meatballs. Cover and cook on low (200°) for 1½ to 2 hours.

LAMB CURRY

This makes a festive dish for company with lots of condiments for embellishing each serving.

2 lb. boneless lamb
1-2 tbs. curry powder
1 tbs. bacon drippings, or olive oil
2 tart apples, peeled and diced
2 onions, chopped
1½ tsp. minced ginger root
2 tbs. flour
2 cloves garlic, minced
1 cup dry red wine

1 cup homemade or canned low fat
  beef broth
1 tsp. lemon juice
salt and pepper to taste
hot steamed rice
toasted almonds, chopped apple,
  crisp bacon, chutney and chopped
  green onion for condiments

In a large skillet, brown meat and curry powder in bacon drippings. Transfer to the crockery pot. Add apples, onions, ginger and flour to skillet and cook until glazed. Transfer to crockery pot. Add garlic, wine, broth, lemon juice, salt and pepper. Cover and cook on low (200°) for 8 to 10 hours. Serve over rice. Pass condiments.

PORK CHOPS IN ORANGE SAUCE

Pork chops gain a shiny, rich glaze and tartness in this sauce.

4 thick center cut pork chops
salt and pepper to taste
1 tsp. olive oil
⅓ cup orange juice
⅓ cup ketchup
1 tbs. orange marmalade
½ tsp. grated orange peel
1 orange, sliced
watercress for garnish, optional

Season pork chops with salt and pepper. In a large skillet, brown well in olive oil. Transfer to the crockery pot. Pour orange juice and ketchup into skillet. Stir in marmalade and orange peel and boil for 1 minute. Pour over pork chops. Cover and cook on low (200°) for 6 to 8 hours. Remove pork chops to a warm platter. Slash orange slices to the center, twist and arrange a slice on each pork chop. Garnish each pork chop with watercress. Pass sauce.

SPINACH AND PORK TERRINE

Here is a brightly ribboned paté, stunning for a party appetizer or first course.

1 pkg. (10 oz.) frozen chopped spinach
¾ lb. lean pork, coarsely ground
1 egg
2½ tbs. cognac, or brandy
2 tbs. chopped fresh parsley
¼ cup finely minced onion
½ tsp. salt
½ tsp. dried thyme

½ tsp. dried basil
¼ tsp. ground nutmeg
¼ tsp. pepper
¼ cup chopped Italian-style olives
4 strips bacon
⅛ lb. boiled ham, sliced
1 bay leaf

Thaw spinach and squeeze dry. Place pork, egg, cognac, parsley and onion in a mixing bowl. Combine salt, thyme, basil, nutmeg and pepper. Add half of seasoning mixture to meat and mix well. Mix remaining seasoning mixture with spinach and olives. Line bottom and sides of a 4-x-7-inch loaf pan (or pan that fits in your crockery pot) with bacon. Spread with ⅓ meat mixture. Cover with ½ spinach; ½ ham slices; another ⅓ meat mixture; remaining spinach, ham and meat mixture. Place bay leaf on top. Cover with foil. Place a trivet in the bottom of the crockery pot and place loaf pan on trivet. Cook in the crockery pot on high (300°) for 2 hours. Chill. Slice to serve.

COUNTRY-STYLE PATÉ

Makes: about 1½ lb. paté
Cooking time: 2 hours

A 1-pound coffee can is the perfect container for baking this sausage-striped paté. Slice it into rounds and serve with sourdough bread as a first course.

3 mild Italian garlic sausages
water to simmer sausages
1 lb. lean pork, coarsely ground
2 slices bacon, ground or finely diced
1 egg
2 tbs. sour cream
2 tbs. minced onion
2 tbs. brandy

1 tbs. flour
2 cloves garlic, minced
½ tsp. grated lemon peel
½ tsp. salt
½ tsp. pepper
¼ tsp. ground allspice
¼ tsp. dried thyme

Place sausages in simmering water in a saucepan for 10 minutes. Drain and cool slightly. Mix together pork, bacon, egg, sour cream, onion, brandy, flour, garlic, lemon peel, salt, pepper, allspice and thyme. Oil a 1-pound coffee can. Spoon ½ meat mixture into can. Poke sausages in vertically. Spoon in remaining meat and pat down. Cover with foil. Place a trivet in the bottom of the crockery pot. Place can on trivet. Cover and cook on high (300°) for 2 hours, or until firm. Allow to cool and chill in the refrigerator.

GLAZED HAM

This easy-to-prepare citrus-mustard glaze uplifts the ham.

5 lb. boneless ham
3 tbs. orange marmalade
1 tbs. Dijon mustard

Trim fat from ham. Mix together marmalade and mustard; spread mixture on top of ham. Place in the crockery pot. Cover and cook on low (200°) for 6 to 8 hours. Transfer ham to a carving board. Pour meat juices into a sauce boat or pitcher. Skim off fat and serve with ham.

HAM LOAF WITH SWEET-SOUR GLAZE

Servings: 8
Cooking time: 3 hours

This meat loaf is excellent hot or sliced cold for sandwiches.

2 cups ground cooked ham
1 lb. lean ground beef
¾ cup quick-cooking oatmeal
1 cup milk
2 eggs
1 tsp. dry mustard
½ tsp. ground ginger

½ tsp. salt
¼ tsp. ground cloves
¼ tsp. ground allspice
¼ cup apple cider vinegar
¼ cup brown sugar, firmly packed
Mustard Sauce, follows

Mix meats, oatmeal, milk, eggs, mustard, ginger, salt, cloves and allspice together. Shape into a loaf, place on a square of foil and lower into the crockery pot. Cover and cook on high (300°) for 2 hours. Meanwhile, boil vinegar and brown sugar in a small saucepan until reduced by half. Cool and spoon over loaf. Continue cooking for 1 hour longer, or until cooked through. Serve with *Mustard Sauce*.

MUSTARD SAUCE

2 tbs. Dijon mustard

¼ cup sour cream

Blend ingredients together.

MEATS 93

TONGUE IN PORT SAUCE

Cooked tongue is delicious glazed with a sprightly wine sauce. Cold, it is a pleasant change for lunch.

1 fresh or smoked beef tongue
1½ cups water
1 bay leaf

1 onion, quartered
6 whole peppercorns
Port Sauce, follows

Place scrubbed tongue, water, bay leaf, onion and peppercorns in the crockery pot. Cover and cook on low (200°) for 7 to 9 hours. Remove from crockery pot and cool slightly. Skin, using a sharp knife. Serve hot with *Port Sauce*. Chill remainder for sandwiches.

PORT SAUCE

⅓ cup ruby port
1 tbs. currant jelly
1 tbs. lemon juice

¾ cup rich beef gravy, or bouillon cube
  plus 1 tbs. cornstarch blended with
  ¼ cup cold water

Combine ingredients and cook, stirring, until thickened. Makes 1 cup.

ITALIAN SAUSAGES IN WINE

Servings: 6 first course, 24 appetizer
Cooking time: 45 minutes-1 hour

Sausages poached in red wine with a spoonful of currant jelly acquire a sensational flavor. Slice them thinly and pass as an appetizer, if you wish, or offer as a distinctive first course to prelude a quiche or cheese soufflé supper.

1 cup dry red wine
2 tbs. currant jelly
6-8 mild Italian sausages, or Polish sausages

Place wine and jelly in the crockery pot. Heat until jelly is dissolved and sauce begins to simmer. Add sausages. Cover and cook on high (300°) for 45 minutes to 1 hour, or until sausages are cooked through and lightly glazed. Transfer to a cutting board and slice thinly for a hot appetizer. Or serve individually in ramekins with juices spooned over.

GLAZED COCKTAIL FRANKS

A crockery pot makes a perfect warmer/server when entertaining. Try this easy appetizer for your next party.

¼ cup Dijon mustard
½ cup dry red wine
¾ cup currant jelly
1 lb. cocktail frankfurters

Combine mustard, wine and jelly in a crockery pot. Heat on high (300°) until hot through, stirring to blend. Add frankfurters and heat to serving temperature. Stir to glaze. Serve with toothpicks or wooden skewers to spear franks.

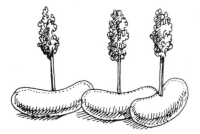

FRANKS IN SPICY TOMATO SAUCE

Makes: 48 appetizers
Cooking time: heat and serve

Here is a fast, hot appetizer that is easy to assemble from ingredients generally on hand.

1 cup ketchup
½ cup brown sugar, firmly packed
1 tbs. red wine vinegar
2 tsp. soy sauce
1 tsp. Dijon mustard
1 clove garlic, minced
1 lb. beef or chicken frankfurters, cut into 1-inch pieces

Place ketchup, brown sugar, vinegar, soy sauce, mustard and garlic in the crockery pot. Cover and cook on high (300°) until blended. Stir occasionally. Add frankfurters and stir to coat. Cook until thoroughly heated. Serve with toothpicks or wooden skewers to spear franks.

PASTA AND CASSEROLES

WHOLE WHEAT SPAGHETTI

Servings: 4
Cooking time: heat and serve

The crockery pot makes an ideal warmer and serving container for this vegetarian-style pasta dish.

8 oz. dried whole wheat spaghetti
2 leeks, white part only, chopped
3 tbs. olive oil
grated peel and juice of 2 lemons
salt and freshly ground pepper to taste
⅓ cup diced oil-cured sun-dried
  tomatoes

⅓ cup oil-cured pitted black olives
2 oz. chèvre cheese, shredded, or
  mozzarella cheese
¼ cup grated Parmesan cheese
¼ cup minced fresh Italian parsley for
  garnish
grated Parmesan cheese for garnish

In a large pot of boiling salted water, cook spaghetti until firm to the bite *(al dente)*, but not too soft or chewy, about 10 to 12 minutes. Drain, reserving about ⅓ cup liquid. While pasta is cooking, sauté leeks in 1 tbs. oil until soft. In a crockery pot, toss together spaghetti, remaining oil, reserved pasta liquid, lemon peel and juice, salt, pepper, leeks, tomatoes, olives and cheeses. Heat to serving temperature. Sprinkle with parsley at the table. Pass Parmesan cheese.

FETTUCCINE WITH SHRIMP AND MUSHROOMS

Servings: 3-4
Cooking time: heat and serve

This delightful pasta entrée makes a great weekend lunch or Sunday supper treat.

8 oz. dried fettuccine
2 green onions, white part only, chopped
1 clove garlic, minced
3 tbs. extra virgin olive oil
½ lb. mushrooms, sliced
1½ tbs. lemon juice

2 tsp. grated lemon peel
⅓ lb. small cooked shrimp
salt and freshly ground pepper to taste
4 oz. whipped or regular cream cheese
fresh Italian parsley and freshly grated Parmesan cheese for garnish

In a large pot of boiling salted water, cook pasta until firm to the bite (*al dente*), but not too soft or chewy, about 10 to 12 minutes. While pasta is cooking, sauté onion and garlic in 1 tbs. oil until soft. Add mushrooms and sauté over medium high heat, stirring, just until glazed. Drain pasta, leaving a little water clinging to it, and place in a crockery pot preheated on low (200°). Toss with remaining oil, lemon juice and peel, shrimp, mushrooms, salt, pepper and cream cheese. Heat through. At serving time, top with parsley and grated cheese.

LINGUINE WITH SMOKED TROUT AND BASIL

Servings: 3-4
Cooking time: heat and serve

This fresh herb and seafood sauce goes together in a jiffy for an elegant pasta first course or entrée. The crockery pot makes a perfect hot serving dish for the table.

¼ lb. smoked trout, or salmon, flaked or diced
¼ cup chopped fresh basil
¼ cup chopped fresh Italian parsley
1 clove garlic, minced
3 tbs. chopped pistachios

3 tbs. diced oil-cured sun-dried tomatoes
salt and pepper to taste
3 tbs. virgin olive oil
8 oz. linguine, or angel hair pasta

In a bowl, combine smoked trout, basil, parsley, garlic, pistachios, tomatoes, salt, pepper and 1 tbs. oil to make sauce. Cook pasta in boiling salted water; drain, reserving ⅓ cup liquid. In a crockery pot preheated on low (200°), toss pasta with remaining oil and reserved pasta liquid. Spoon trout-basil sauce on top.

ANGEL HAIR PASTA WITH CLAMS

Servings: 3-4
Cooking time: heat and serve

This is a fast entrée that holds nicely if some family members are late.

2 tbs. olive oil
4 shallots, chopped
2 cloves garlic, minced
1/2 cup clam juice, or fish or chicken broth
1/4 cup vermouth, or dry white wine
1/4 cup heavy cream
1/2 lb. shelled whole cooked clams, or mussels or canned whole clams

2 tbs. chopped fresh basil
2 tbs. chopped fresh parsley
salt and freshly ground pepper to taste
1/2 lb. angel hair pasta
1/3 cup freshly grated Parmesan cheese for garnish
fresh basil sprigs for garnish

In a large skillet, heat oil and sauté shallots and garlic until soft. Add clam juice and vermouth and reduce by half. Add cream and reduce slightly. Add clams and heat through. Season with basil, parsley, salt and pepper. In a large saucepan, cook pasta in boiling salted water. Drain, reserving 1/3 cup liquid. Place in a crockery pot on low (200°) and toss with sauce. Sprinkle with Parmesan cheese and serve with a few basil sprigs.

FETTUCCINE ALFREDO

Servings: 6
Cooking time: heat and serve

The Roman restaurant, Alfredo, makes a flourish of serving this pasta dish. Look for fresh egg noodles in the refrigerated section of your market.

3 tbs. butter
1 cup heavy cream
¾ cup shredded Gruyère cheese
1 cup shredded Parmesan cheese, or Romano cheese
16 oz. fresh egg fettuccine

Melt butter in the crockery pot. Add cream, Gruyère cheese and half the Parmesan cheese. Heat on high (300°) until bubbly. Cook noodles in boiling salted water until firm to the bite (*al dente*), but not too soft or chewy. Drain and rinse in a colander under cold running water. Add well-drained noodles to sauce. Stir and toss to coat completely. Sprinkle with remaining cheese and heat to serving temperature.

SPAGHETTI CARBONARA

Servings: 6
Cooking time: heat and serve

A crockery pot is an ideal warmer/server for this renowned Italian pasta entrée. The hot pasta cooks the egg yolks and melts the cheese.

¼ lb. bacon, diced
1 bunch green onions, chopped
1 tsp. olive oil
2 egg yolks
½ cup finely chopped fresh cilantro, or fresh parsley
1 cup diced fontina cheese, or Gruyère cheese

⅔ cup shredded ham, or prosciutto
1 lb. spaghetti, vermicelli, homemade noodles or fettuccine
seasoned pepper for garnish
1½ cups grated Parmesan cheese for garnish

In a large skillet, sauté bacon until crisp. Drain on paper towels. Remove fat from skillet. Sauté onions in oil until limp. Beat egg yolks. Have ready bacon, egg yolks, cilantro, diced cheese and ham, each in a separate bowl. Cook spaghetti in boiling salted water. Drain and transfer to a crockery pot preheated on low (200°). Mix in bacon, egg yolks, cilantro, diced cheese and ham. Pass pepper and grated Parmesan cheese.

RAVIOLI CASSEROLE

Servings: 8
Cooking time: 1 hour

This is a delicious dish that only takes 1 hour of cooking in the crockery pot.

1 pkg. (10 oz.) frozen chopped spinach
1 pkg. (8 oz.) spiral pasta
1 lb. ground beef chuck
½ lb. mild Italian sausage
1 onion, finely chopped
1 tsp. olive oil
2 cans (8 oz. each) tomato sauce
salt and pepper to taste

1 tsp. dried oregano
½ cup shredded Parmesan cheese,
 or Romano cheese
1 cup (½ pt.) sour cream
1 cup (4 oz.) shredded Monterey Jack
 cheese
3 green onions, chopped

Defrost spinach and squeeze dry. Cook pasta in boiling salted water. Drain. In a large skillet, brown meats and onion in oil, until meats are crumbly. Add tomato sauce, salt, pepper and oregano. Cover and simmer for 30 minutes. Mix in spinach. Spoon half of cooked pasta into a buttered crockery pot. Top with half of meat mixture and Parmesan cheese. Cover with layers of remaining pasta, meat and Parmesan cheese. Spread with sour cream and sprinkle with Jack cheese and onions. Cook on high (300°) for 1 hour.

VEAL AND ARTICHOKE CASSEROLE

Servings: 6
Cooking time: 2 hours

Tender chunks of veal and distinctively flavored artichoke hearts are simmered in a delicious tomato-wine sauce.

2 lb. veal stew meat, cut into 1½-inch pieces
1 tsp. olive oil
1 onion, chopped
2 tomatoes, peeled and diced
3 cloves garlic, minced
1 cup homemade or canned low fat chicken broth

1 cup dry vermouth
salt and freshly ground pepper to taste
1 tsp. dried basil
2 pkg. (9 oz. each) frozen artichoke hearts, thawed
1 tbs. white wine vinegar
3 tbs. chopped fresh parsley for garnish

In a skillet, sauté veal in oil until browned. Add onion and cook until glazed. Transfer to a crockery pot. Add tomatoes, garlic, broth, vermouth, salt, pepper and basil. Cover and cook on high (300°) for 2 hours, or until meat is almost tender. Add artichoke hearts and vinegar and cook for 30 minutes longer. Sprinkle with parsley.

TIAN

This ratatouille casserole is traditionally baked in an earthenware "tian."

1 small eggplant, diced
salt to sprinkle on eggplant
1 tsp. olive oil
1 red onion, chopped
1 red bell pepper, seeded and cut into
  1-inch chunks
4 Roma tomatoes, sliced
2 zucchini, or yellow squash, cut into
  ½-inch slices

¼ cup dry red wine
2 tbs. tomato paste
1 tsp. chopped fresh thyme
1 tsp. chopped fresh basil
salt and freshly ground pepper to taste
¼ cup freshly grated Parmesan cheese,
  or Romano cheese
¼ cup pine nuts
fresh basil sprigs for garnish

Place eggplant in a colander, sprinkle with salt and allow to drain for 30 minutes; rinse and pat dry. In a large skillet, heat oil and sauté onion and pepper for 5 minutes. In a crockery pot, alternate layers of eggplant, sautéed vegetables, tomatoes and zucchini. Add red wine and tomato paste to skillet and stir to loosen browned bits. Pour over vegetables and sprinkle with thyme, basil, salt and pepper. Scatter cheese and nuts over mixture and cook on high (300°) for 1½ to 2 hours. Garnish with basil.

CHICKEN, MUSHROOM AND ARTICHOKE CASSEROLE

Servings: 6
Cooking time: 8 hours

These three main ingredients make a tasty combination.

1 broiler-fryer chicken, about 3 lb., cut in pieces
salt and pepper to taste
1/2 tsp. paprika
1 tbs. olive oil
1/2 cup rich chicken broth
3 tbs. dry sherry

1 tsp. fresh tarragon, or 1/4 tsp. dried
1/4 lb. mushrooms, sliced
1 tbs. cornstarch
1 tbs. cold water
1 can (15 oz.) unmarinated artichoke hearts, drained

Wash chicken. Pat dry with paper towels. Season with salt, pepper and paprika. In a large skillet, brown chicken in 1 tsp. olive oil. Transfer to the crockery pot. Pour broth and sherry into skillet and stir to loosen browned bits. Pour over chicken. Season with tarragon, cover and cook on low (200°) for 8 hours. Just before serving, sauté mushrooms in remaining oil until glazed. Combine cornstarch with water. Turn crockery pot to high (300°). When sauce is simmering, stir in cornstarch mixture. Cook until thickened. Add sautéed mushrooms and artichoke hearts. Heat and serve.

CHOUCROUTE GARNI

This Alsatian sausage and sauerkraut dish makes a splendid one-dish meal. Dijon mustard is a must for a condiment.

1½ qt. sauerkraut, about 3 lb.
2 slices bacon, diced
2 onions, finely chopped
4-6 regular pork chops, or smoked
  pork chops
2 tart apples, peeled and diced

2 cloves garlic, minced
8 whole peppercorns
1 cup dry white wine
2 lb. assorted sausages: mild Italian
  sausages, bratwurst or kielbasa

Place sauerkraut in a strainer, rinse under cold water and drain well. In a large skillet, sauté bacon with onions and pork chops until meat is browned. Place sauerkraut and apples in a crockery pot. Arrange pork chops and onions on top. Add garlic, peppercorns and wine. Cover and cook on low (200°) for 4 to 6 hours. Add sausages and cook for 1 hour longer.

TOSTADA PIE

Good companions for this entrée are Mexican beer, avocado and tomato salad, and fresh pineapple wedges.

Meat Sauce, follows
2 tbs. butter, or margarine, softened
4-6 corn tortillas
1½ cups (6 oz.) shredded Monterey
  Jack cheese
½ cup sour cream
2 green onions, chopped

Prepare *Meat Sauce.* Place a square of foil in the bottom of a crockery pot. Lightly butter one side of each tortilla. Lay 1 tortilla, buttered side up, on foil. Spread with a layer of *Meat Sauce* and a layer of cheese. Cover with another tortilla, more *Meat Sauce* and cheese. Repeat layers ending with cheese. Cover and cook on high (300°) for 1 hour. When ready to serve, lift from crockery pot by foil corners. If desired, slip into broiler to brown cheese. Cut in wedges. Combine sour cream and onions and serve with tostada pie wedges.

MEAT SAUCE

1 tsp. olive oil
1 onion, chopped
1 lb. lean ground beef or turkey
½ tsp. salt
½ tsp. dried oregano
¼ tsp. hot red pepper flakes
2 cloves garlic, minced
1 can (8 oz.) tomato sauce
1 cup sliced pitted black olives

In a skillet, heat oil and sauté onion until golden. Add ground beef, Mexican seasoning, salt, oregano, pepper flakes, garlic and tomato sauce. Cover and simmer for 30 minutes, or transfer to a crockery pot and cook on low (200°) for 8 hours. Mix in olives.

ITALIAN MEAT SAUCE

Spoon this sauce over tagliarini or spaghetti, or use it in pasta dishes such as lasagna. Blended with ricotta cheese, it makes a choice filling for cannelloni.

2 onions
2 carrots
2 stalks celery
1 tsp. olive oil
1 lb. ground pork
1 lb. ground veal, or lean ground beef
3 cloves garlic, minced

4 tomatoes, peeled and chopped
1 cup dry red wine
2 tsp. dried basil
2 beef bouillon cubes
salt and pepper to taste
1/4 cup heavy cream

Grate onions and carrots. Finely chop celery. Sauté in oil in a large skillet until glazed. Transfer to a crockery pot. Brown meats in skillet, crumble with a fork and transfer to crockery pot. Add garlic, tomatoes, wine, basil and bouillon. Cover and cook on low (200°) for 8 hours. Skim fat. Season with salt and pepper and stir in cream. Cook on high (300°) until reduced to desired consistency.

CASSOULET

This French country bean casserole is a natural for a crockery pot.

1½ cups small white or great Northern
 beans, soaked overnight, drained
4½ cups water
3 slices bacon, diced
2 medium onions, chopped
1 lb. boneless lamb, cut into 1-inch
 pieces
1 lb. pork shoulder, cut into 1-inch
 pieces

1 cup dry red wine
2 tbs. tomato paste
½ cup beef stock
1 carrot, peeled and grated
2 cloves garlic, minced
1 tsp. dried thyme
salt to taste
1 lb. mild Italian sausage pieces, or
 other sausages, sliced diagonally

Simmer beans in 4½ cups water for 1 hour. Drain and place in the crockery pot. Sauté bacon and onions in a large skillet until golden. Transfer to crockery pot. In the same skillet, brown lamb and pork in remaining drippings. Transfer to crockery pot. Pour wine, tomato paste and stock into skillet. Stir to loosen browned bits. Add to crockery pot with carrot, garlic, thyme and salt. Cover and cook on low (200°) for 6 to 8 hours. Add sausages and cook for 1 hour longer. Arrange sausages on top of casserole before serving.

FRUITS AND DESSERTS

Fresh fruits poach or bake beautifully in a crockery pot and can be the basis for great desserts or everyday breakfast treats. The cooking time will vary with their ripeness and variety, so be sure to check the crockery pot frequently (often by just peering through the see-through lid) to verify doneness.

You can also cook wonderful preserves in your crockery pot. The real joy of making jams, marmalades, chutneys and fruit butters the crockery pot way is that they simmer to the proper consistency without scorching and without the need for frequent stirring. Thicker preserves can be achieved by cooking for several hours on low (200°) with the cover removed.

Finally, it is possible to make quick breads and cakes in your crockery pot — you may prefer not to heat the oven, or you may be in a location without an oven, and having a crockery pot makes baking possible. Before baking, select a mold or can that fits your crockery pot and is the correct size for the recipe you are using. A 1- or 2-pound coffee can, a pudding mold or 2 small loaf pans stacked at an angle may work for you.

APPLES BAKED IN WINE

A rosy wine glaze makes a pretty sauce for plump baked apples.

4 Rome Beauty or Golden Delicious apples
1 orange
½ cup rosé wine
⅛ tsp. ground nutmeg
⅓ cup light brown sugar, firmly packed
frozen yogurt or ice cream for topping

Core apples. Peel off ring around top. Arrange in the crockery pot. Remove 2 strips orange peel with a vegetable peeler. Cut orange in half and squeeze out juice. Add peel, juice, wine, nutmeg and brown sugar to crockery pot. Cover and cook on low (200°) for 3 or 4 hours, or until apples are fork-tender. Cool. Serve with frozen yogurt or ice cream.

CINNAMON SPICED APPLESAUCE

Tart, first-of-the-season Gravenstein or Pippin apples make superb applesauce.

8-10 large cooking apples
½ cup water
½-¾ cup sugar
1 tsp. ground cinnamon
light cream, optional

Peel, quarter and core apples. Place in the crockery pot. Add water and sugar and sprinkle with cinnamon. Cover and cook on low (200°) for 8 hours (or on high at 300° for 3 to 4 hours). Serve warm or cold with cream, if desired.

SHERRIED APRICOT COMPOTE

Apricots plumped in wine are refreshing over vanilla ice cream.

1 lb. dried apricots
2½ cups water
¼ cup brown sugar, firmly packed
½ cup pale dry sherry
½ cup golden raisins, or dried currants
juice of 1 lemon
vanilla ice cream or frozen yogurt
¼ cup toasted slivered almonds

Place apricots, water, brown sugar, sherry, raisins and lemon juice in the crockery pot. Cover and cook on low (200°) for 3 to 4 hours, or until fruit is plumped. Cool. Serve scoops of vanilla ice cream or frozen yogurt in dessert bowls. Spoon on sherried apricots. Sprinkle with nuts.

APRICOTS AND CARAMEL CRUNCH SUNDAES

Caramelized almonds lend a crunchiness to this apricot dessert.

1 qt. fresh apricots, halved and pitted
¼-½ cup brown sugar, firmly packed
3 tbs. water

vanilla ice cream or frozen yogurt
Caramelized Almonds, follows

Layer apricots in the crockery pot. Sprinkle brown sugar between layers. Add water. Cover and cook on low (200°) for 1 to 2 hours, or until apricots are just tender. Serve warm, spooned over scoops of vanilla ice cream or frozen yogurt. Top with *Caramelized Almonds*.

CARAMELIZED ALMONDS

2 tsp. butter
2 tbs. sugar
½ cup slivered or sliced almonds, or chopped hazelnuts

Heat butter and sugar in a skillet until melted. Add nuts and sauté, shaking pan, until nuts are glazed with caramelized sugar. Turn out onto foil to cool.

GINGERED BAKED PAPAYA

Hot spiced papaya makes an intriguing fruit accompaniment to roast chicken, duck or pork. It is a festive dessert as well, accompanied by pineapple or champagne sherbet.

2 small or 1 large papaya
2 tbs. butter
1½ tbs. lime juice
2 tsp. grated ginger root, or ½ tsp. ground ginger

Cut small papayas in half (if large, cut into quarters). Scoop out seeds. Combine butter, lime juice and ginger in a saucepan. Heat until butter is melted. Arrange papaya pieces in the crockery pot and spoon gingered butter into each cavity. Cover and cook on high (300°) for 1½ to 2 hours, or until tender. Baste once or twice with butter mixture. Serve hot.

PEACHES MELBA-STYLE

Poach fresh peaches and drench with raspberry sauce for a delectable dessert.

1 cup sugar
1½ cups water
1-inch piece vanilla bean
6 large fresh peaches
1 pkg. (10 oz.) frozen raspberries, thawed
1 qt. vanilla ice cream

Place sugar, water and vanilla bean in the crockery pot. Heat on high (300°) until sugar is dissolved and syrup comes to a boil, about 45 minutes. Peel and halve peaches and add to hot syrup. Simmer for 15 to 20 minutes, or until fruit is tender. Remove from heat and cool in syrup. Puree raspberries and press through a sieve to remove seeds. Serve poached peaches in bowls with scoop of ice cream on each. Pass raspberry sauce to pour over ice cream.

RUBY PEARS

Baste pears occasionally so they absorb the wine juices and turn ruby red.

1 cup dry red wine
1/3 cup sugar
4-6 Bartlett pears, or Bosc pears
4-6 whole cloves

Stir wine and sugar together in the crockery pot. Heat on high (300°) until sugar dissolves. Remove cores from pears. Leave peel and stem intact. Stud each pear with a clove and place in crockery pot. Cook on low (200°) for 3 to 4 hours (or on high for 1½ to 2 hours). Baste occasionally. Serve warm or chilled.

FRESH PLUMS IN PORT

Spicy wine flavors permeate poached plums thoroughly after chilling. Slash plums on one side to pit.

1 orange slice
4 whole cloves
1 qt. whole pitted purple prune plums
1 cup ruby port
½ cup sugar
1 whole cinnamon stick

Quarter orange slice and stud with cloves. Place in the crockery pot with plums, port, sugar and cinnamon stick. Cook, uncovered, on high (300°) until sugar is dissolved. Turn temperature to low (200°). Cook for 1 hour, or until fruit just begins to soften. Transfer to a covered container. Chill.

ORANGE-PLUMPED PRUNES

Cook prunes overnight, if you like, for a hot breakfast fruit.

1 lb. large pitted prunes
1 cup orange juice
1 whole cinnamon stick
1 lemon, thinly sliced

Place prunes, orange juice and cinnamon stick in the crockery pot. Arrange lemon slices on top. If necessary, add a little more juice or water to just cover prunes. Cover crockery pot and cook on low (200°) for 8 hours, or until prunes are plumped.

RHUBARB BERRY SAUCE

Accompany with light cream or ice cream for a refreshingly light fruit dessert.

2 cups fresh strawberries, or 1 pkg. (10 oz.) frozen whole strawberries, thawed
butter-flavored nonstick vegetable spray
1 qt. rhubarb, thinly sliced
¾ cup sugar
3 tbs. minute tapioca
1 tsp. grated orange peel
¼ cup water
light cream, frozen yogurt or ice cream

Wash and hull strawberries. Spray the crockery pot with nonstick vegetable spray. Place strawberries and rhubarb in crockery pot. In a bowl, blend sugar, tapioca, orange peel and water together. Add to crockery pot and mix lightly with fruit. Allow to stand for 15 minutes. Cover and cook on low (200°) for 3 to 4 hours, or until fruit is just tender when pierced with a fork. Serve with light cream, frozen yogurt or ice cream.

ORANGE STRAWBERRY SUNDAES

Orange juice and ruby port are old-time favorites with strawberries. For a shortcake-style dessert, serve over slices of pound cake. When strawberries are out of season, substitute with 6 oranges.

2 oranges, peeled
1 can (6 oz.) frozen orange juice concentrate
1¼ cups ruby port
2 cups hulled strawberries
1 qt. vanilla ice cream or frozen yogurt

Peel, halve and thinly slice oranges. Heat orange juice concentrate and port in the crockery pot on high (300°). When bubbling, add oranges and strawberries. Heat just until hot, about 10 minutes. Serve in crockery pot, allowing guests to spoon over scoops of ice cream or frozen yogurt.

SUMMER FRUIT COMPOTE

A medley of late summer fruits is poached in lemon-scented honey for this colorful dessert.

12 plums
2 peaches
6 apricots
1/4 lb. green or red seedless grapes
1/3 cup sugar

1/2 cup water
1 tbs. honey
1 tbs. lemon juice
1 lemon, thinly sliced
yogurt, sour cream or light cream

Wash, halve and seed plums, peaches and apricots. Wash and stem grapes. Combine sugar and water in a saucepan. Bring to a boil and cook until sugar is dissolved. Stir in honey and lemon juice. Place prepared fruit in the crockery pot. Add syrup. Arrange lemon slices on top of fruit. Cover and cook on low (200°) for 6 hours (or on high at 300° for 1½ to 2 hours). Cool slightly or chill before serving. Serve in bowls. Pass yogurt, sour cream or light cream.

APPLE CIDER BUTTER

Makes: about 8 cups
Cooking time: 5½ hours

Brown sugar lends a caramelized richness to this smooth apple butter.

5 lb. cooking apples
1½ cups apple cider
3 cups brown sugar, approximately,
  firmly packed
juice and grated peel of 1 lemon

juice and grated peel of 1 orange
2 tsp. ground cinnamon
1 tsp. ground allspice
½ tsp. ground cloves
¼ tsp. ground nutmeg

Core and quarter apples, but do not peel. Place in the crockery pot with apple cider. Cook on high (300°) until very soft, about 1½ hours. Press cooked apples through a food mill or sieve. Measure — there should be about 6 cups. For every 1 cup fruit pulp, allow ½ cup brown sugar. Return to crockery pot. Stir in remaining ingredients. Cover and cook on high (300°) until thick and dark, about 4 hours. Immediately pour into hot, sterilized jars and seal.

FRUITS AND DESSERTS   129

ORANGE MARMALADE

Makes: about 5 pints
Cooking time: 3¾ hours

When winter navel oranges are at their prime, use them for this beautiful, bright orange marmalade.

6 oranges
water to cover oranges

½ cup lemon juice
6 cups sugar, approximately

Remove peel from 4 oranges. Place peel in a saucepan, cover with water and simmer for 30 minutes. Lift out cooked peel. Reserve water. Using a spoon, scrape off the white membrane from cooked peel and discard. Slice and chop orange peel. Peel remaining 2 oranges and thinly slice all 6 oranges. Place sliced oranges, peel and reserved water in the crockery pot. Add lemon juice and enough additional water to cover just ⅔ of fruit. Cover and cook on high (300°) for 1 hour. Measure and return to crockery pot. Turn off heat. Stir in sugar, allowing 2 cups sugar for each pint of fruit. Allow to stand for 2 hours. Stir occasionally. Without covering crockery pot, bring mixture to a boil on high. Boil until mixture reaches the jelly stage (it will sheet from a spoon), about 15 minutes. Ladle into hot, sterilized jars and seal.

APRICOT PINEAPPLE JAM

Makes: about 9 cups
Cooking time: 1-2 hours

Pineapple lends a delightful sweetness to contrast with the tang of apricots in this classic jam.

2½ lb. fresh apricots, about 7 cups sliced
1 can (15 oz.) crushed pineapple
5 cups sugar

Wash and slice apricots. Place in the crockery pot with pineapple and sugar. Cook on high (300°), uncovered, until thickened, about 1 to 2 hours. Stir occasionally. Ladle into hot, sterilized jars and seal.

RHUBARB STRAWBERRY JAM

Makes: 4 pints
Cooking time: 2¼-3¼ hours

This jam is a beautiful color. Spoon it over toasted English muffins for breakfast.

2 lb. rhubarb
6 cups sugar
2 lb. strawberries, about 4 cups mashed

Wash rhubarb. Cut into ½-inch pieces and place in the crockery pot. Cover with sugar and allow to stand for 2 to 3 hours. Turn crockery pot to high (300°) and bring to a boil. Add strawberries and cook just until thickened, about 15 minutes. Ladle into hot, sterilized jars and seal.

APRICOT CHUTNEY

Makes: 4 pints
Cooking time: 4-6 hours

This colorful chutney is delicious with lamb curry, roast duck or turkey.

1 qt. ripe apricots, chopped
2 cups chopped firm ripe apricots
1 large onion, grated
10 cloves garlic, minced
1 cup vinegar
1 can (8 oz.) crushed pineapple
2 tsp. salt
1½ cups brown sugar, firmly packed

2 tsp. dry mustard
1 tsp. ground cinnamon
½ tsp. ground cloves
½ tsp. ground allspice
dash cayenne pepper
1 tsp. grated lemon peel
⅓ cup sliced crystallized ginger
¾ cup slivered blanched almonds

Place apricots, onion, garlic, vinegar, pineapple, salt, brown sugar, mustard, cinnamon, cloves, allspice, pepper, lemon peel and ginger in the crockery pot. Cover and cook on low (200°), stirring occasionally, for 4 to 6 hours. Remove cover, add nuts and cook on high (300°) until desired consistency. Ladle into hot, sterilized jars and seal.

GINGERED PLUM CHUTNEY

Makes: about 3 pints
Cooking time: 4-6 hours

Here is another sprightly fruit chutney, so good with game and broiled or curried meats.

1 qt. fresh Italian prunes
1 cup sugar
1 cup light brown sugar, firmly packed
3/4 cup apple cider vinegar
1 1/2 tsp. hot red pepper flakes
2 tsp. salt

2 tsp. mustard seed
3 cloves garlic, minced
1/4 cup grated onion
1/2 cup thinly sliced preserved ginger
1 cup golden raisins

Halve and pit prunes. Place sugars, vinegar, pepper, salt, mustard seed, garlic, onion, ginger and raisins in the crockery pot on high (300°) until sugar is dissolved. Add prunes. Cook on low (200°) for 4 to 6 hours. Stir occasionally. If desired, remove cover and cook down to desired consistency. Ladle into hot, sterilized jars and seal.

WHOLE GRAIN DATE BREAD

Slice this enriched date bread into rounds and spread with cream cheese.

1 cup boiling water
1 cup chopped pitted dates
3 eggs
1 cup brown sugar, firmly packed
½ cup all-purpose flour
½ cup whole wheat flour

¼ cup wheat germ
1 tsp. baking powder
½ tsp. baking soda
½ tsp. salt
2 cups all-bran cereal
1 cup coarsely chopped pecans

Pour boiling water over dates. Cool. Beat eggs until light. Add brown sugar and beat until thick. Stir in dates. Combine flours, wheat germ, baking powder, soda and salt. Add to egg mixture and beat just until blended. Blend in cereal and nuts. Pour into a well-greased 1-pound coffee can and cover top of can with 4 layers of paper towels. Put a trivet in the bottom of crockery pot and place can on trivet. Place crockery pot lid on loosely, allowing steam to escape. Cook on high (300°) for 3 hours, or until a toothpick inserted into the center comes out clean.

ORANGE PECAN BREAD

Makes: 1 loaf
Cooking time: 3½-4 hours

Spread thin slices with sweet butter.

¼ cup butter
1 cup sugar
1 egg
2 cups all-purpose flour
1 tsp. baking powder

1 tsp. baking soda
½ tsp. salt
1 cup orange juice
1 cup chopped pitted dates
½ cup chopped pecans

Cream butter and sugar. Beat in egg. Combine flour, baking powder, soda and salt. Add dry ingredients to creamed mixture alternately with orange juice. Blend until smooth. Add dates and nuts. Pour batter into a greased, floured 2-pound coffee can. Place can on a trivet in the crockery pot. Cover can with 4 to 5 paper towels. Place crockery pot lid on loosely so steam can escape. Cook on high (300°), allowing 3½ hours for a 3½-quart crockery pot and 4 hours for a 4½-quart crockery pot, or until a toothpick inserted into the center comes out clean. Cool on a wire rack for 10 minutes. Remove from can and cool.

WHEAT GERM BROWN BREAD

Makes: 1 large loaf
Cooking time: 4 hours

Steam this moist brown bread in a 2-quart mold or a 3-pound coffee can. This bread freezes well.

1 cup whole wheat flour
1 cup all-purpose flour
1 cup yellow cornmeal
½ cup wheat germ
1 tsp. baking powder
1 tsp. baking soda
1 tsp. salt

½ cup brown sugar, firmly packed
¼ cup dark molasses
3 tbs. soft butter
2 cups buttermilk
1 cup golden raisins
2 cups water

Place flours, cornmeal, wheat germ, baking powder, soda, salt and brown sugar in a mixing bowl. Stir until blended. Add molasses, butter and buttermilk. Beat until dry ingredients are moistened. Stir in raisins. Transfer batter to a greased, floured 2-quart pudding mold or a 3-pound coffee can. Place a trivet in the bottom of the crockery pot. Pour water into crockery pot. Place filled mold or can in crockery pot. Cover top with foil, extending it to cover top of crockery pot. Cover and cook on high (300°) for 4 hours, or until a toothpick inserted into the center comes out clean.

WHOLE WHEAT BANANA BREAD

Wheat germ and walnuts lend a nutty flavor to this moist fruit bread.

⅔ cup butter
1 cup sugar
2 eggs
1 cup pureed bananas
1 cup whole wheat flour

1 cup all-purpose flour
¼ cup wheat germ
½ tsp. salt
1 tsp. baking soda
½ cup chopped walnuts, or pecans

Cream butter with an electric mixer. Add sugar and beat until smooth. Add eggs and banana puree. Beat until smooth. Blend flours, wheat germ, salt and soda. Add to creamed mixture. Beat just until smooth. Transfer batter to a well-greased 1-pound coffee can. Place on a trivet in the crockery pot. Cover coffee can with 4 paper towels. Place crockery pot lid on loosely to allow steam to escape. Cook on high (300°), allowing 3½ hours for a 3½-quart crockery pot and 4 hours for a 4½-quart crockery pot, or until a toothpick inserted into the center comes out clean.

CHOCOLATE HAZELNUT CAKE

Mashed potatoes lend moistness to this old-fashioned chocolate nut cake.

⅔ cup butter
1½ cups sugar
4 eggs
1 cup mashed potatoes
2 cups all-purpose flour
⅔ cup unsweetened cocoa

2 tsp. baking powder
1 tsp. salt
1 tsp. ground cinnamon
½ cup milk
½ cup chopped hazelnuts, or pecans
 or walnuts

Cream butter. Beat in sugar and eggs until smooth. Mix in cooled potatoes. Combine flour, cocoa, baking powder, salt and cinnamon. Add dry ingredients to creamed mixture alternately with milk. Add nuts. Transfer batter to a greased, floured 3-pound coffee can or 3-quart pudding mold. Cover top of can with 4 layers of paper towels. Place can on a trivet in the crockery pot. Place crockery pot lid on loosely so steam can escape. Cook on high (300°) for 3½ to 4 hours, or until a wooden skewer inserted into the center comes out clean. Cool on a wire rack for 10 minutes. Remove cake from can or mold.

CHOCOLATE CHIP SOUR CREAM CAKE

Makes: 1 large cake
Cooking time: 4-5 hours

A decorative mold works well for this delectably moist cake.

1/2 cup butter
1 cup sugar
2 eggs
1 cup (1/2 pt.) sour cream
1 tsp. vanilla extract

2 1/2 cups all-purpose flour
1 tsp. baking powder
1 tsp. baking soda
1/2 tsp. salt
1 pkg. (6 oz.) chocolate chips

Cream butter and sugar. Add eggs and beat until smooth. Mix sour cream and vanilla. Stir flour, baking powder, soda and salt together. Add to creamed mixture. Stir in chocolate chips. Transfer to a greased, floured 2 1/2- to 3-quart mold or 3-pound coffee can. Place on a trivet in the crockery pot. Cover top of mold with 4 layers of paper towels. Place crockery pot lid on loosely so steam can escape. Cook on high (300°) for 4 to 5 hours, or until a wooden skewer inserted into the center comes out clean.

BEER SPICE CAKE

Your guests will be surprised at the secret ingredient.

⅔ cup butter
1½ cups brown sugar, firmly packed
2 eggs
2½ cups all-purpose flour
1½ tsp. baking powder
½ tsp. baking soda

¼ tsp. salt
1 tsp. ground cinnamon
1 tsp. ground allspice
1 can (12 oz.) beer, or 1½ cups
½ cup chopped walnuts
½ cup golden raisins

Cream butter and brown sugar until light. Beat in eggs. Combine flour, baking powder, soda, salt, cinnamon and allspice. Add dry ingredients to creamed mixture alternately with beer. Mix until blended. Stir in walnuts and raisins. Transfer batter into a well-greased, floured 2-quart pudding mold or coffee can. Place on a trivet in the crockery pot. Cook on high (300°), allowing 3½ hours for a 3-quart crockery pot and 4 hours for a 4½-quart crockery pot. Cool on a wire rack for 10 minutes before removing cake from mold or can. Serve warm with *Hard Sauce*, page 143, or ice cream.

STEAMED CARROT PUDDING

Servings: 6
Cooking time: 4-5 hours

This steamed pudding makes a gala finale to a holiday feast.

1 cup all-purpose flour
1 cup brown sugar, firmly packed
1 tsp. baking soda
1 tsp. ground cinnamon
1 tsp. ground allspice
1/2 tsp. ground cloves
1/3 cup butter, softened
1 egg
1 cup grated carrots
1 cup grated apples, or potatoes
1/2 cup golden raisins
2 cups water
Hard Sauce, follows

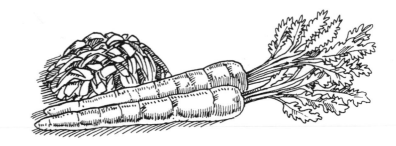

Place flour, brown sugar, soda and spices in a mixing bowl. Stir to blend. Add butter and egg. Mix until smooth. Stir in carrots, apples and raisins. Transfer batter to a greased, floured 2-quart coffee can and cover with foil. Set a trivet in the bottom of the crockery pot. Pour 2 cups water into crockery pot. Set coffee can on trivet and cover crockery pot with foil. Put lid on crockery pot. Cook on high (300°) for 4 to 5 hours, or until a toothpick inserted into the center comes out clean. Serve warm with *Hard Sauce*.

HARD SAUCE

¼ cup butter
1 cup powdered sugar
2 tbs. honey

Beat butter until creamy. Beat in powdered sugar and honey.

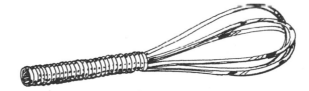

MOROCCAN APPLESAUCE CAKE

Makes: 1 large cake
Cooking time: 3-3½ hours

Serve this unusual cake warm with scoops of coffee or chocolate ice cream or frozen yogurt.

½ cup butter
1 cup sugar
2 eggs
1 tsp. vanilla extract
1 cup applesauce
1½ tsp. baking soda

1½ cups all-purpose flour
1 tsp. ground cinnamon
½ tsp. salt
1 cup chocolate chips
¾ cup chopped dates, or raisins
¾ cup chopped walnuts

Cream butter and sugar. Add eggs one at a time. Beat until smooth. Add vanilla. Combine applesauce and soda, and stir in. Mix flour, cinnamon and salt. Add to creamed mixture and beat until smooth. Mix in chocolate chips, dates and walnuts. Transfer batter to a greased, floured 2-quart pudding mold or 2-pound coffee can. Place on a trivet in the crockery pot and cover with 4 layers of paper towels. Place crockery pot lid on loosely so steam can escape. Cook on high (300°) for 3 to 3½ hours, or until a toothpick inserted into the center comes out clean.

HOT BEVERAGES

A crockery pot works admirably as a beverage warmer/server for a crowd. It is festive and practical for a wintertime party. Guests can serve themselves at will and the hot beverage stays at a perfect temperature without the host or hostess's attention. Conveniently prepared ahead of time, the flavor improves as the ingredients slowly steep together.

DILLED TOMATO COCKTAIL

Dill pickle juice punctuates this quick tomato beverage.

3 cups tomato juice
2 tsp. sugar
½ tsp. celery salt
1 clove garlic, minced
1 tbs. Worcestershire sauce
dash liquid hot pepper sauce
½ cup dill pickle juice
popcorn, or croutons, for garnish

Combine tomato juice, sugar, celery salt, garlic, Worcestershire sauce, hot pepper sauce and pickle juice in the crockery pot. Heat on low (200°) for 1 to 2 hours. Ladle into mugs. Sprinkle a few kernels of popcorn on each serving.

CITRUS SPICED TEA

Hot citrus-scented tea is a welcome beverage for a winter afternoon party.

3 qt. water
1/3 cup tea leaves
1½ cups sugar
1 tbs. whole cloves
1 tsp. whole allspice
2 whole cinnamon sticks
4 lemons
3 oranges

Heat 2 qt. water to boiling. Remove from heat. Add tea, cover and steep for 10 minutes. Strain into the crockery pot. Add sugar, cloves, allspice and cinnamon. Heat on low (200°) until sugar is dissolved. Remove peel from 2 lemons and 2 oranges with a vegetable peeler. Add to crockery pot. Squeeze juice from fruit. Strain and pour into crockery pot. Add remaining water and heat until steaming hot.

HOT SPICED CIDER

Here is a spicy mulling of cider, wine and oranges.

½ gal. apple cider
2 cups chablis or fruity white wine
4 oranges, sliced
2 whole cinnamon sticks
12 whole cloves

Place cider, wine, oranges, cinnamon and cloves in the crockery pot. Cover and heat on low (200°) until hot. To serve, remove cover and ladle into heatproof punch cups.

SWEDISH GLÖGG

Typical of Scandinavian festivities is this richly spiced wine punch. In Sweden it is traditional to ignite a large lump of sugar and brandy and let it flame into the hot wine. Any remaining glögg may be poured into jars or wine bottles and stored in the refrigerator for future use.

1 gal. port
1-2 cups brandy, or bourbon
1 tbs. whole cloves
1 tbs. peeled cardamom pods
3-4 whole cinnamon sticks
1 cup dark raisins

Place port and brandy in the crockery pot. Wrap cloves, cardamom and cinnamon in cheesecloth. Add to crockery pot. Stir in raisins. Heat on low (200°) until steaming hot.

HOT MULLED WINE

Another Swedish variation of hot wine punch is based on dry red wine. You have the option of using either vodka or brandy for the spirits.

1½ cups sugar
3 cups water
1 whole cinnamon stick
6 cardamom pods, peeled
12 whole cloves
½ cup golden raisins
¼ cup blanched almonds

¼-inch slice ginger root, optional
1 lemon, thinly sliced
½ gal. dry red wine
1-2 cups vodka or brandy
golden raisins and blanched almonds
  for garnish

Combine sugar and water in a saucepan. Bring to a boil. Heat, stirring, just until sugar is dissolved. Pour into the crockery pot. Add remaining ingredients. Heat on low (200°) until steaming hot. Ladle into heatproof punch cups or mugs. Be sure each cup gets an almond and a few raisins.

INDEX